VOICES OF
NATIVE AMERICA

NATIVE AMERICAN INSTRUMENTS
AND MUSIC

by

DOUGLAS SPOTTED EAGLE

*"This book is Dedicated to Tom Bee and to all who have ever
Heard and Appreciated the Rhythms of the Earth"*

Eagle's View Publishing
A WestWind Incorporated Company
6756 North Fork Road
Liberty, UT 84310
801/745-0905 - Voice
801/745-0903 - Fax
PorsTurbo@aol.com

ISBN 0-943604-56-7
Library of Congress Catalog Card Number 97-60768

FIRST EDITION

OTHER EAGLE'S VIEW BOOKS BY DOUGLAS SPOTTED EAGLE

HOW TO MAKE INDIAN BOWS AND ARROWS...THE OLD WAY
HOW TO MAKE ARROWS...THE OLD WAY

B0029 - 12 11 10 9 8 7 6 5 4 3 2 1

TABLE OF CONTENTS

ILLUSTRATIONS

ILLUSTRATIONS

ILLUSTRATIONS

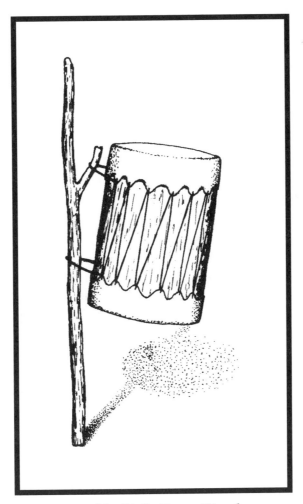

Pueblo Style Drum Stand

ACKNOWLEDGEMENTS

The author wishes to gratefully acknowledge the people in his life who made this publication possible; foremost, my publisher, Monte Smith and his partner, Denise Knight. I know they spent hundreds of hours and gallons of coffee making the edits and corrections in this writing possible. All illustrations were done by Monte "Smitty" Smith, of *And Frames, Too* of Salt Lake City, Utah; his work makes a fine addition to all of my books.

Linda, Josh, Amanda, John, thanks for always being a part of my life, my mother and father, Tom Bee and the SOAR family, Robert Jones, Louise Dee, Derek Mathews and the people at the Gathering of Nations, Doug and Susan at Q-Up Arts, the boys in Indian Creek, Eastern Eagle, Blacklodge, Medicine Hoop, Sons of Ogalala, Babe New Holy, Sharon Arrowchis, Sam Moves Camp, all the flute players out there, the fans that have supported not just my music, but all Native music. Skip Webb, Pete Yellowjohn, Wil Numkena, Julian Bee, Davis Mitchell, Jay Begay, Cathedral Lakes Singers, Yamarika, Baldwin Duncan, Jim Bilagody, Brian Keane and Ron Bach. Special thanks to Kim, Steve and the community of Stockton. You all have taught me something, and my life is better for knowing you. There are so many more drum groups and Native musicians not listed here, as space will not permit. We could do a whole book of Native musicians who have touched and bettered my life.

[1] - Photos on Pages 88 (White Snow Goose Whistle of Carved Wood) and 89 (Crane's-head Whistle) are used with the permission of Bob Scriver from his wonderful book, *The Blackfeet: Artists of the Northern Plains.*

[2] - Pictures on Pages 81 (Traditional Crow Rattle) and 85 (Tin Cone Leg Shaker) are used by permission of the Denver Art Museum from their *Persistent Vision* Collection.

The photo of the author on Page 4 was taken by Bill Reinert.

All photos of the Soar Recording artists were taken by Robbie Bee.

Please visit our website at - www.spottedeagle.com

This book was produced on a Power Macintosh with Jaz, Zip and Bernoulli drives. Graphics were provided by RT Computer Graphics from their *The Plains Collection* and *The Santa Fe Collection.*

FOREWORD

The Wasi'cu have seemingly been fascinated with Native American culture from the moment that the Pilgrims first set foot on our island. Names of states, regions, books, films, television, clothing, and various "ism's" have all been based in part, at times, on Native culture.

Unfortunately, most students and fans of Native America only see a small portion of what our culture is really about; particularly that of the musical existence of our peoples. And music is really one of our most defining characteristics.

Our music is dynamic. It still has very traditional forms, but is evolving rapidly. There are Native traditionalists, rappers, country artists, rockers, folk singers, jazz players, instrumental artists, and many, many more, all of whom bring their traditional Native backgrounds into their music. These artists are more than just Native people making music; they are bringing an accessibility to music that non-Indians rarely have had in the past 50 years. As a result of this access, Native influences are being heard in all forms of music recorded by non-Indian people.

From the viewpoint of someone who has been involved with the popularization of Native music since the beginning of recorded music, this book is much needed. What few writings that do currently exist are written by musicologists, not musicians involved with Native music. And Sir Thomas Beecham describes a musicologist as *"a man who can read music, but can't hear it"*. (Beecham Stories/1978). For this reason, most who study Native American music hear nothing but wordless, seemingly meaningless chants, when in truth, tremendous emotion and deliverance is taking place. Whether the sounds are actual depictions of specific thought, or simply emotional performances, these sounds all come to us from the Creator. This is truly what Native music is all about. And I hope this book helps the reader to discover this truth. Nina was'te doh.....

Nitawa Kola
Tom Bee

TOM BEE

ABOUT THE AUTHOR

Douglas Spotted Eagle is a musician, dancer, singer, producer, recording engineer, writer, and craftsman. As a musician, he is known as one of the most preeminent performers with the Native American flute, having his flute voice and percussion heard on over ten million records and videos. His music and sounds have been heard on such projects as *The X Files*, *Star Wars Ewok* cartoon series, *Johnny Quest*, *500 Nations*, several Disney, HBO, Showtime, TNT, and TBS special programs or series, and many other projects to date. He has performed for or with individual greats such as Willie Nelson, Robbie Robertson, Peter Buffett, Craig Chaquico, and David Arkenstone, and has (at the time of this writing) eleven solo records. Through his developed CD Rom, Douglas has produced and provided sounds for hundreds of artists, including Michael Jackson and Mark Isham. He has recorded for several major recording labels, such as Capitol, Narada, Windham Hill, Epic, and Elektra.

As a producer, Douglas has produced over 200 pow wow and other forms of Native music including NAC/peyote, country, rap, new age, rock, and spoken word. His recording group, Native Restoration, has developed recording techniques for live pow wow recordings that have changed the face of not just recorded pow wow music, but the techniques in large area sound reinforcement at pow wows as well.

Together with Tom Bee from SOAR Records, Douglas produced the very first compact disc release of pow wow music, taking Native music into a very new and powerful market and changing the face of Native music forever. His *Sacred Feelings* was the first flute recording ever to be heard in the new digital medium as well.

"Spot", as Douglas is nicknamed, has always tried to approach Native music in the same manner as a large name recording group would be approached, even in it's most raw traditional form. As a result of this approach, he became a staff producer for Sound of America Records early in his career. Armed with these tools, he quickly became immersed in the many forms of Native American music.

Soundtrack work for film is also another format in which Spot's work may be heard. His soundtrack to *Naturally Yours* won a Telly award, HBO's *Paha Sapa* was nominated for an Emmy Award, and BBC's *White Birds of Winter* was nominated for a British television award. His distinctive sound is heard in *The Scarlet Letter* (starring Demi Moore) *Squanto*, *On Deadly Ground*, and dozens of other large screen productions

This book is his third foray into the literary world, having written two books at the ages of nineteen and twenty, respectively, relating to Native American archery. *Voices of Native America* is a result of his many years of recording, production, performance, and involvement with various

aspects of Native music all over the United States and Canada.

Douglas Spotted Eagle and his family currently reside in the small desert community of Stockton, Utah, where he raises horses and makes music at the Native Restoration recording studio.

DOUGLAS SPOTTED EAGLE

AN OVERVIEW OF NATIVE AMERICAN MUSIC TODAY

Native American music has recently become one of the most listened to, influential, and cultural forms of music in the world today. Several films have received awards for music inspired by, or directly recorded from, indigenous cultures. However, this being said, it must be pointed out that Native music varies tremendously in form, style, and presentation. Traditional and contemporary artists create rock, rap, funk, trance/dance, country, new age, acappella, symphonic, religious and hard core traditional.

Until the late 1960's, Native music was something only heard on museum recordings or at cultural events. There were no books relating to Native music, except in museum studies, and music used in film up to that time was entirely an Anglo interpretation of what Native America "sounded like." This is particularly true of the stereotypical and farcical *Drums Along the Mohawk* rhythms. The cultural explosion of the 60's era caused musicians of several musical forms to begin to take a closer look at what influences might make their music more individual. Bands such as XIT, Redbone, Buffy St. Marie, and others, were discovered by major record companies, like Motown and Capitol. Motown artist XIT became uncommonly popular as the anthem group of the American Indian Movement (AIM) during their sieges at Wounded Knee and Alcatraz. The media favorably reported the 'rebel' music, creating tremendous waves in the Indian music industry. Independent record companies spawned new ground for traditional groups as well, not to mention the surge of contemporary artists such as Buddy RedBow and Wil Numkena, with over one hundred traditional and contemporary recordings available by 1980. Pow wows, trading posts, and mountain man gatherings became primary outlets for the recordings and Europe was a major breaking ground for top Native artists. It didn't take long for the American market to catch on to what was happening.

In the mid 1980's, Native flautists, performing on traditional instruments, caught the public ear. Tom Machaughty-Ware, R. Carlos Nakai, Kevin Locke, and many others, became celebrated performers in the Native world, and thus Native American music joined the New Age movement. Nakai, at the time of this writing has sold over 2 million records. Today, film, television documentary, and multi-media presentations the world over have indigenous influences found in their soundtracks.

Although Native music has always been available in some form since the beginnings of recorded media, major changes took place in the late 80's and early 90's. Prior to that time, Native music was relegated to cheap cassettes, stick on labels, and Xeroxed or one color covers. Some recordings had been released on vinyl, though, at that time, very few. In fact, most of the recordings were mono rather than stereo. Indian House, Indian Sounds, Canyon Records, Sunshine Records (Canada) and Highstar had all been in business and distributing Native American recordings for some time, but the envelope was yet to be pushed.

SOAR Records, a relative newcomer to the indigenous music scene, changed the future of Native music forever. In 1988, Tom Bee, the former leader of the popular Native American rock group XIT, began the label in his garage, hocking his watch and overcharging his credit cards. Generating multi-color graphics, using high bias or *Digalog*™ tapes, and selling door to door out of the back of his truck, SOAR Records

was born. Not only did Bee take a major label approach to indigenous music, he also had the courage to release the first commercial Native recording on compact disc. Since that time, new labels and current competitors have begun to do the same, bringing Native music in all forms to an extremely marketable level. Needless to say, SOAR Records is no longer in a garage, nor being sold out of the back of a truck. Tom Bee is also now known as the "Father of contemporary Native music', and has earned the Will Sampson Achievement in the Arts Award.

Native music is timeless, both in it's

XIT

inception and contemporary medium. The music comes from the earth; from the heartbeat of our Mother. From the time that our early ancestors began to communicate with the earth, through the use of drums, to the time that the flute was given to the people, the music has been a major participant in ceremony and daily life. Voices in both "straight" and word form have accompanied dances and ritual since the beginning of time, even today. The basic rhythms have not changed, only the voices and words. True, modern music forms have influenced the vocal structures,

RUSSELL MEANS

PAUL LAROCHE

ROBBY BEE

TIGER TIGER

JULIAN B.

CORNEL PEWEWARDY

even to the point of harmonies being found from time to time among modern drum groups, yet the overall styling and arrangements of the songs are the same today, as they were hundreds of years ago.

An old Lakota story tells of a time when a voice was heard out in the hills, just as darkness was falling, and the dusk stars were showing themselves. It was a man's voice, and so the People looked throughout the camp to see who was missing, and, therefore, know who the voice belonged to. No one was missing. All of the People in the camp began to walk towards the sound, circling the hill as they did so. Upon completing the circle around the hill, the People could see that the one singing was a coyote, not a man. It was in this way that they learned the songs, and continue to sing those songs today.

The majority of traditional music falls into two general categories; social and religious. Religious music has been primarily left out of this text for reasons of respect. It is not that these songs, styles, or words are secret, but because they are sacred. As with any tool, used by someone uninitiated to it's uses, the sacred songs could be potentially dangerous.

The social songs, while heard at numerous events, are particularly used at pow wows. The word pow wow is Anglicized from the Algonquin word *pau-au*, meaning "gathering of holy men and spiritual leaders." Non-Indians eventually mispronounced and misused this word, causing it to eventually become a word defining any gathering of Native peoples; and, at times, a serious meeting between Indians and non-Indians. As the various Nations became more familiar with the English language, they too, accepted this word for a social gathering. The concept of what pow wow has become is originally a Plains assembly, and now symbolizes unity among Native Nations across the continent. A pow wow is being held somewhere almost every weekend of the year at some place across the country. Pow wows are held for celebration, for holidays, to honor veterans and elders, for memorials, fund raisers, birthdays, and simply just to have one. The pow wow is a spiritual experience without being a religious one. It allows the people to re-touch their roots, to share a moment with others, to dance in appreciation for who they are. Dancers, at these celebrations, honor the drums that bring good music to them, allowing them to physically and emotionally express the feelings that the music calls out from their lives.

Social songs heard at pow wows may be divided into two groups: Northern style and Southern style. At one point in time, geographical region defined who sang what songs. In contemporary times, men from the south often sing northern style songs,

and men from the northern areas also sing southern style songs.

There are several styles of traditional singing, each having it's own place in the spectrum. Despite the various styles in songs, they all can be broken down into two groups of presentation. Word songs, or songs performed with actual words in either Native language, sometimes even English. These songs are dropping by the wayside among many Northern vocal groups. One theory behind this is that so many songs are shared by various nations, that it becomes too difficult for singers of one nation to learn the word forms of another nation. Consequently, straight songs, or songs sung without actual words, but rather "vocables" such as *heyneyyana* or *wheenanoheeyee* become the primary structure of the vocal rhythm. Some older traditionalists have labeled the newer forms of straight songs as "potato chip songs", referring to the fact that without words, the song may not have meaning, or being "high fat, low sustenance." Others feel that the newer forms of singing are

merely part of the dynamic of the culture, and are changing in a manner consistent with all of life. Perhaps it could be said that the message carried by the more modern forms of singing is based on emotion, rather than literal delivery.

The old ones say that the five fingered mind cannot comprehend the Creator, nor understand the world as the Creator intended it to be. Therefore, songs that express these things that are not completely understood, are sung with emotional syllables, or non-descriptive words. How might one describe the sound of running water, the wind in the trees, the smell of the blue in the sky? Perhaps the use of the word "Hallelujah" in Christian melody ascribes to the same thought process.

Many of the contest songs today use a mix of tribal language and vocables, urging the dancers to move "quickly, surely, and to dance, dance, dance." This style is rapidly catching on, and is heard from some of the extremely popular groups in the pow wow circuit.

Some songs are considered to be for religious use only, such as sundance, Yuwipi, Stomp dance, or harvest songs. These songs should not be used outside of their specific function, lest harm fall to those who sing them in an improper place. No record company or person with any degree of integrity should record or release these songs out of respect for those that have need for strength in the song. Although the author has personally recorded over two hundred Native American record projects, never has a sacred song been recorded by the author.

The Native American Church has it's own form of song, generally referred to as "peyote" music. Only recently have recordings of this vocal form been found, yet they

are gaining in popularity very quickly.

Peyote songs are sung with a water drum, a gourd, and one or several singers. As with most forms of traditional vocals, the first singer will generate the melody, with others joining in with the first repeat, or "push-up". Between each repeat, the drum is retuned by allowing the water inside the drum to rewet the drum head. The drum is played by only one person, who places the drum on the floor. The drum is 'retuned' or rewet at each turnaround by splashing water inside the drum against the head of the drum. All of this is done with the drum never stopping its rhythm. A gourd player keeps a steady beat going in sixteenth notes, with the drum beat in eight. At the end of each repeat, the gourd is rapidly shaken, in nearly 32nd counts

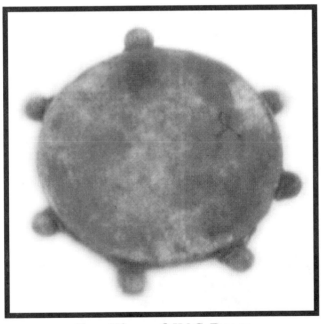

Top View of NAC Drum

on the "3 and", with the gourd quickly going back to eighth counts on the down beat. Solo performers of this style will often hold a gourd in the same hand as the drum stick, playing both drum and gourd at the

same time. Although the 'cascade' or rapidly shaken gourd is not heard at the end of a verse, this method allows the gourd to be heard, and in perfect time with the drum. Typical cadence for a peyote song is about 140 beats per minute, making the songs quite fast. Most often the songs have 4 repeats or pushups.

Contemporary Native American Church singers have begun to add harmonies in recent years, most notably Primeaux and Attison, Guy and Allen, and Jay Begay. In some instances, the use of drum, rattle, or both, adds a more spiritual and free quality to the voice. Some of the newer harmonized songs are sung free, or without the rhythmic control of the drum and gourd, with the song being performed acapella. The elders say that the old Lakota way of singing these songs was harmonized, and over time the harmonies were forgotten. It is wonderful to hear them coming back.

As mentioned above, traditional drum groups heard at powwows today have two basic forms of singing; it is the Northern Traditional style whose songs tend to begin higher in pitch and more melodic in harmonic structure. Many of the younger drum groups seem to be drawn to this form of singing, and it is here that rock and roll influences are most commonly heard. Many of the songs heard at pow wows are Northern in style, and until recent times, most recorded songs were also Northern, so Northern styles of songs are easily available. While not unheard of, it is rare to find women around the drum singing with the men. The changing dynamic due to the popularization of Native music in the past fifteen years is bringing new forms to the music. In older times, it would be common for women to stand around a drum,

Ute social gathering circa 1900.

singing with the men. Generally speaking, however, women do not strike the drum.

Southern Traditional drums sing at a lower pitch with a more stabilized melodic

structure, and tend to become very powerful as the song progresses through its' repeats. Southern Traditional style singing is heard at powwows all over the country, and at all gourd dances, held to honor

Piegan dance 1922 Note drum group in lower right hand corner

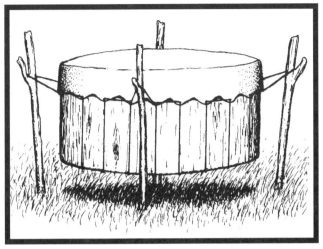

Plains Style Drum Support

veterans and families of veterans. It is common for women to sing with the men at a Southern style drum. The women generally sing an octave above the men but it is rare for women to actually sit at the drum using a stick on the drum, although in contemporary times it is becoming more common.

In either northern or southern styles of singing, the form is largely the same. The leader starts the vocal, with a second singer following up his first vocal line with a slightly altered repeat. The rest of the

The Author is pictured here (center of the photo in striped shirt) with contemporary drum group, Eastern Eagle.

Drum group at a Recording Session

singers join in to sing the rest of the chorus. Honor beats, or heart beats, indicate the end of a chorus and beginning of a verse. Dancers often dip their heads or raise their hands during these 'turn-arounds' in honor of the drum. The end of the song is generally marked by a slight increase in tempo, volume, and off beats at the last 5 beats of the chorus. Some drum groups sing a 'tail' or repeat of the chorus without the lead verse, and the song is finished. Competitive dancers must finish on the beat, or be disqualified from the competition.

Traditional drum groups utilize only a large round drum, generally made from a standard bass drum frame with all of the metal hardware removed, and horsehide, cowhide, or elk hide being used for the skin. Most drums are covered top and bottom, suspended between four posts. This allows the drum to develop more bass tones, and ring with no interference. No shakers, gourds, or other instruments are used, with the dancers providing the eighth count rhythms.

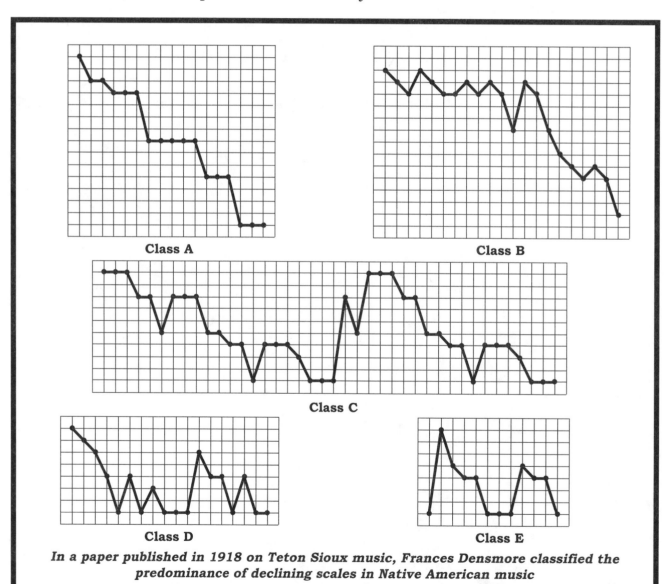

Class A

Class B

Class C

Class D

Class E

In a paper published in 1918 on Teton Sioux music, Frances Densmore classified the predominance of declining scales in Native American music

The entire group, generally consisting of 4 to 16 singers/drummers, sit around the drum. All drummers have sticks similar in weight and length and all members of the group drum. The powerful sound of 16 sticks hitting a 28 inch drum is difficult to imagine, and must be heard in person to appreciate. It is substantially more powerful than even the largest of taiko drums, with the strongest of drummers; it is perhaps the acoustic equal of an amplified rock kick drum. Also unique in contemporary singing are the heartbeats, or honor beats, struck at various points in the song, generally during a turnaround, or pushup, but these beats can be heard through other points in the song as well, punctuating a lyric or phrase. Most drum groups as a rule have two or three persons designated to deliver these heartbeats, giving the drum an additional life. The number of singers varies only on personal relationships, as friends of the drum groups will often join in, and share in the song, making the vocals more powerful. In older times, typically there were only three to four singers, and by all reports, they were nearly as powerful in the past as today with larger numbers of singers.

It is most common for the group to have one or two lead singers that establish the melodic structure of the song, with all members of the group joining in at the second line of the song. Some drum groups, particularly the southern drums, have women standing next to the seated singers, sing-

Song of the Grass Dance

Kills at Night

An example of Declining Scale

Black Face Paint He Grants Me

Red Bird

Wakan Tanka ca wa ki ya___ can na i th sa bye maku___ welo___

Another example of Declining Scale

ing an octave above the drum group, giving the drum an even more powerful voice.

The melodic structure of most traditional format songs are in a declining scale, beginning the melody at a high note, cascading down to an octave or a minor third below the initial note. This cascade may take several turns in a short space, but regardless of the melodic structure of the song, in nearly all cases, the melody ends on an octave below the beginning point.

Song classifications can be broken down into several rhythmic styles. Each style lends itself to a particular dance form. "Two step", sometimes known by other names such as rabbit dance, or owl dancing, depending on the geographical region, is played in a 2 beat time, with the accent coming on the '2' rather than the one count. "Crow Hop" is essentially the same beat, with a different vocal time, and the accent generally on the "1". Northern Men's, Southern Men's, Northern Women, Buckskin and Cloth, Ladies Fancy, and Ladies Jingle Dress are all basically the same rhythm, with only the vocal timing changing. Southern Fancy, or Omaha dancing, is generally performed with a fast Southern Drum, about 120 bpm - often with tricky stops and starts written into the song. "Trick" songs are just what the name implies. The rhythm of the song may change from sixteenths to eighths, to quarter beats, with varying tempos. The object of the song is for the drum group to be able to trick the dancers into moving their feet when there is no struck beat.

Flag songs, honor songs, and retreat songs vary tremendously with each drum group. Each group may have their own style of bringing in downbeats, starts and repeats.

The flag song is sung following the

grand entry at a powwow, when all the dancers are in the arena, and circling the eagle staff and flag(s). The flags represented may be the American flag, the POW flag, VFW flag, state flag, tribal or nation flag, etc. The flag song is to honor all present, Native and non-Native alike. The flag and song represent those who have gone be-

fore; our ancestors. When the flag song is sung, the audience remains standing after the grand entry, and the dancers stand in place. There is no dancing during a flag song, as the song belongs to the flag and to nothing and no one else. A retreat song is played after the flag song, and it is appropriate to dance at that time.

"Shake" songs change in tempo and rhythm just like trick songs, but the object of the song is not to trick the dancers, but rather to give them an opportunity to shake their jingles and feathers, making sure that all accouterments are firmly attached, and that nothing will fall off during a competition. Having an eagle feather fall off of a dance outfit is embarrassing at the least, and requires a veteran to pick up the feather, and a song from a drum group to help the veteran pick the feather off the ground. It is no more appropriate for a feather to lay on the ground, than it is for an American flag to lie on the ground.

Only a veteran may pick up a fallen feather, as the feather is representative of a fallen comrade. The veteran will approach the feather 3 times "attempting" to recover it. On the fourth approach, he will pick up the feather, and hold it in the air to show that it has been successfully recovered. The feather is then given back to the dancer, who may give the feather to the veteran, the drum group, or keep it for him/herself. It is also customary for the dancer who has lost the feather to pay both the veteran(s) and the drum group participating in the ceremony. The payment does not so much represent a financial appreciation of the effort, but rather a personal sacrifice on the part of the dancer who has made the mistake of allowing a feather to drop to the ground.

Dancers wear feathers in their dance roach or hair for a variety of reasons, but one of the stories relating to why the dancer wears feathers, is that one day while a warrior was dancing, an eagle saw the dance, and appreciated the warrior for sharing his feelings with the earth, and those around him. The eagle made an offering of one of

his tail feathers to the dancer, to show his appreciation for the dance. The feather was dropped from high above, where it floated

Example of Feathers in a Head Roach

down to the earth. As the dancer reached his hand high in the air to indicate his thankfulness for the Creator above, the dropped feather landed in his hand.

In order for the reader to best understand some of these songs, rituals, and practices, a powwow should be attended. Powwow's are large social gatherings, with everyone welcome. However, if the reader has never attended a pow wow, there are some rules of etiquette that must be observed. First, never take a photo of a dancer without their permission. The dancer may feel 'somehow' about having their picture taken. Do not point with an index finger at a dancer. It is rude, and impolite. Use the lips or eyes to point. Do not touch any part of a dancer's regalia. It may be considered a religious offense, or merely impolite. It takes many years and dollars to obtain the materials needed to make an outfit, and in the hands of the uneducated, the materials may be damaged or destroyed. While intertribal dances are for everyone present, contests and honor dances are for contestants and those being honored, and those wishing to acknowledge those being honored. Finally, do not cross the arena floor in front of dancers. Go around the room, or arena, to arrive at your destination. To do otherwise is disrespectful of the dancer, the arena, and the culture.

Outside of the pow wow arena, during the pow wow, other forms of music are heard going on as well. For instance, you

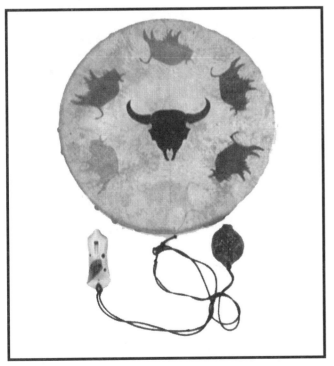

Ute Handgame Hand Drum

may hear handgame songs. This game involves two teams of players, one hiding a small marked bone or stick, and the other team guessing who has the stick concealed. Similar to "hide and seek," this game has a rapid rhythm of drum, singing, and sometimes rattles. At some handgames, people have been observed using unopened boxes of macaroni and cheese as rattles!! The songs are fast, humorous, and fun. Most times gambling on the teams is encouraged and expected, albeit that the wagers on this ancient game are usually small.

Forty niner songs are also heard late into the night around reservation pow wows, and the songs generally contain words about a lost love, begging a young lady to accompany a young man home for the evening, or light sexual humor.

The Dine' (Navaho) people have a social dance called the "Squaw Dance", where the rhythm is moderate (approximately 120 bpm) and the dance involves both men and women dancing together. The song style is similar to 'song and dance', and the contemporary performers of song and dance are just as loved on the reservation as Elvis is in non-Native culture. A particularly well known performer is Davis Mitchell, who at one concert, even had women throwing clothing at him!

The water drum is used much in the same way as it is used by the Native American Church but without the gourd rattle. The dance tempo is also much slower. The water drum, in this case, is held while standing, rather than placed on the ground.

Song and Dance evolved from the "Squaw Dance," as the song and dance is a social dance for men and women, and "squaw" dance is more related to younger women asking men to dance. Squaw dance is a significant part of a seven day cer-

DAVIS MITCHELL

emony. The young women ask the men to dance, and the male is expected to pay the young women a small payment for the dance; e.g., a dollar or so.

A social gathering similar to line dancing or square dancing, Song and Dance is for men and women, married or single. The men dress in their best silver and turquoise jewelry complete with bandolier bags, polished boots, and velvet shirts. The women also dress in their finest silver, turquoise, velvet, and moccasins. The dance is similar to a two step, with arms interlocked, and one foot swung forward in time with the down beat. These social dances can go on all night. At these social gatherings, men are not expected to pay the women with whom they dance. Some Song and Dance gatherings sponsor contests, with the winners taking home money, food, blankets, sheep, or cloth. There are also contests between song and dance performers, either individual, or between song and dance groups.

The Tlingit, Kwakiutl, and Nootka peoples of the Northwest Coast have a social gathering called a 'potlatch", from the Nootka word *patshatl* meaning "to give." The potlatch comes with it's own set of songs, in honor of those giving to the community.

Among the Creeks and Cherokees, Stomp Dance also has it's own various songs and accompanying rhythms, as does the Sun Dance of the Plains, Flute Ceremonies of the Hopi, Hako Ceremony of the Pawnee, and so many other dances, ceremonies, and rituals, that encyclopedias could be filled documenting the musical styles of over 900 various nations on this continent. With that in mind, there are several ceremonies and rituals that are not specifically named within these pages. This is not due to a lack of importance, but

A Mixed Song and Dance Group

rather that the sheer number of events would create an entire book. Also, most music for ceremonial/ritual performance will follow the designated patterns and forms found in this book.

Indigenous music is changing everyday. With major record labels signing Native artists, or Native-influenced artists, and greater outlets for ethnic music, the current trend towards a 'world' beat, and larger numbers of Native youth turning to music as an expression of their national pride insure this change. The increase in world communications due to the Internet, television, radio, greater distribution of compact discs worldwide, and heightened interest in non-European cultures assures that the dynamic changes in Native American and Native influenced music will continue for many generations to come.

A Male Only Song and Dance Group

FLUTES

"There has always been a flute, just as there always have been young people. The flute is as old as this world....."

For many years, this instrument has been by far my favorite instrument. It is the only instrument truly indigenous to North America, as there are no similar two chambered instruments that have been found on any other continent, past or present. While the drum plays an integral role in Native culture, it is an instrument found on all continents, used by all peoples, as is the shaker, whistle, rattle, Apache-style violin, bull roarer, and rasp.

The flute is an instrument primarily related to emotional expression, both in contemporary and traditional times. In the past, young men used the flute to steal the heart of their favorite young lady. Even in contemporary times, from a traditional perspective, only males play the flute. Some Nations have used the flute in some aspect of ritual, although the flute has historically been known for it's amorous qualities.

It has often been suggested that the flute follows early European influence. Under no circumstance can this be true, as flutes have been scientifically found to date back 2000 years, long before Amerigo Vespucci or Columbus claim to have set foot on this island of North America. While the number of holes, tunings, and the specific styles of the flute have evolved, the basic instrument has remained the same.

Nearly all nations of this continent have historically had flutes, either of their own manufacture, or obtained from other nations. Many of the eastern nations used birch bark or willow with the wood removed while the sap would allow the inner section to be slipped. The Seminole created flutes of bamboo, without a manufactured stop, using the natural "breaks" found inside the shoot. Yuma and other southwestern nations used cane much in the same way as the Seminole, yet the "saddle" would be flush with the mouthpiece end of the flute body, thus eliminating the air chamber. Museum pieces show that the Mandan created a flute or pipe similar to the pan pipes of the Andeans by tying eagle quills together in double rows. Kwakiutl and Tlingit's used dual tone reed whistles, as did many other Northwestern nations.

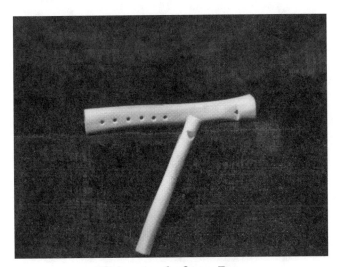

Flutes made from Bone

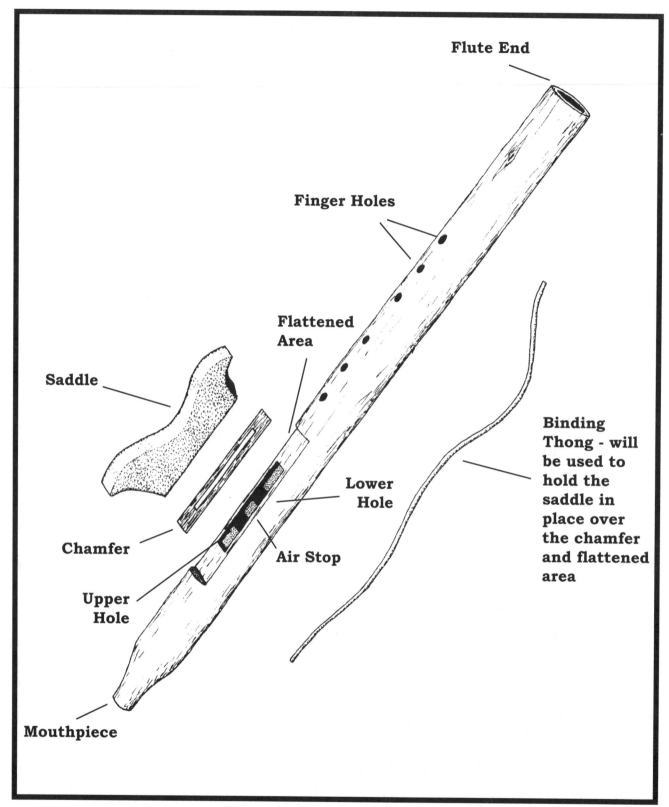

Flute End

Finger Holes

Flattened Area

Saddle

Binding Thong - will be used to hold the saddle in place over the chamfer and flattened area

Chamfer

Lower Hole

Air Stop

Upper Hole

Mouthpiece

The Parts of a Flute

Sacred ritual in the Southwest called for a fingered whistle made from a large eagle quill. The Zuni created flutes from clay, and, while the Plains nations are famous for their flutes of cedar, modified gun barrel flutes were not at all uncommon. Ironic that a weapon of destruction might be converted to a weapon of emotion.

Traditional style flutes have four basic components; an air chamber, a tonal chamber, a saddle to assure properly directed air movement, and tone holes.

The air enters the first chamber, where it meets a stop, or block of material preventing air movement into the next chamber. The air then seeks the path of least

resistance, which is a hole drilled at the top end of the first chamber. Upon leaving the first chamber, the air encounters a saddle, or block, which may either have a chamfer carved in it, or it may rest upon a wood or metal air guide. This block/chamfer device directs the air into a hole drilled

at the top beginning of the second air chamber. The second hole is angled into the inner section of the flute body as shown in the illustration.

Depending on the geographical region, the number of finger holes, or notes, will vary from four to seven holes. The Hidatsa speak of "the old woman who never dies" cutting a section of sunflower stalk for her grandson. She cut seven holes in the stalk to represent the seven months of winter. When he blew on the stalk, snow would fly from the seven holes. Often times the flutes will also have two or four holes drilled in the end of the flute body. These end holes, similar to Chinese flutes, serve no purpose other than that of decoration. These flute holes are found on most of my personal flutes as a recognition of the four directions.

The length of the flute is determined in modern times by the desired key. The lower the key, the longer the flute. A G minor below middle C is as long as 42 inches, while a G minor above middle C is only 16 inches in length. In more traditional terms, the flute length would be determined by measuring the distance from the tip of the index finger to the "bone" of the elbow, or about 20 inches. In contemporary terms, this would create a flute roughly in the key of F# or G.

The diameter of the flute is also determined by the desired key. A G minor flute (below middle C) is approximately 2 3/4 inches in diameter, while it's counterpart two octaves higher is less than 3/4 of an inch in diameter.

Hole size is generally between 1/4 inch and 3/8 inch. The flute may be roughly tuned by slightly enlarging the holes, beginning with the upper, or higher holes. A traditionally tuned flute is difficult at best to blend with contemporary instruments with any strict degree of harmony, but by working with the various distances between the holes, length and diameter of the flute, an instrument with highly accurate 'concert' tuning is possible.

(Author's Note: The following section is a discussion, in general terms, of the make-up of a flute. For specific, step-by-step instructions on how to make a flute, please see the next Chapter, *Making a Native American Flute*.)

In order to make a flute, begin with a rounded piece of wood, cut to the desired length. (For the beginning flute maker, creating a working instrument should be the goal, rather than attempting to create a concert masterpiece.) Cedar, white pine, walnut, nearly any wood is great for making a flute. The harder the wood, the more mellow the flutes tone will be. Try to select wood that is knot-free in the lower portions of the wood. Using a table saw or band saw with a guide, split the wood exactly in half. If the goal is to make the flute in a traditional manner, use a knife to carefully split the wood, making sure that the wood does not splinter along any portion of the edge.

Draw a line marking the lower section and upper section on each piece. The block should be approximately 1/4 inch thick.

Hollow the lower section of each half using a chisel, gouge, or power drill with a round rasp head. A Dremel™ tool is also a great choice, or a router in a steady hand. Carve the wood on each length to an equal thickness. If the lower section has areas thicker or thinner than other areas, then the wood will not resonate well, and will not sound as balanced as it should. The walls of the flute should be no thicker than

1/4 inch at any point.

Carve out the wood on the upper area in the same manner as the lower area was carved. Extra care must be taken to assure that the marked out section for the block is not damaged, as any air escaping through the block will negatively affect the tone and performance of the flute.

Using sand paper or a chunk of sandstone, clean the inside areas well, so that they are smooth and even, unsplintered and clear.

Once the inside areas of the flute are prepared, determine which piece will be the top piece. Set the bottom piece aside. Drill a hole 1/4 inch in diameter on both sides of the uncarved stop or block. The hole nearest the mouthpiece will remain as it is drilled, while the hole on the "finger side" will need to be filed at an angle.

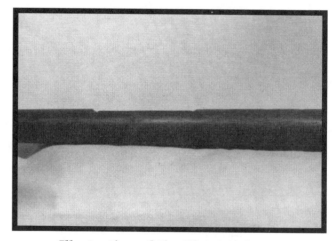

Illustration of the Flattened Area

Before filing the angle, "flatten" out the rounded body of the flute 1/2 inch behind and ahead of the two air holes drilled in the top of the flute body. This will create a base for the saddle, and give an equal thickness to the front hole when the angle is filed properly. The angle properly channels the air into the lower chamber, mak-

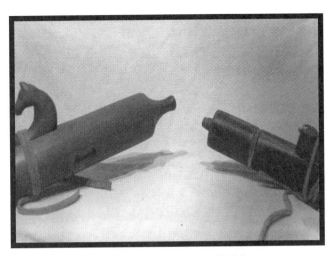

Examples of the Mouth Piece
(Flute on the left courtesy of Scott Loomis)

ing the tone of the flute more rich and clear.

Now the mouthpiece must be made by either using the chisel to create a small valley in the mouth ends of each section or by putting the two sections together, fastening them tightly, and drilling a 3/8 hole in the joint, equally dividing the hole between each section.

The saddle is the object that sits on top of the flute, responsible for directing the air from the upper section of the flute into the lower section. Saddles are also known as "birds," "blocks" and "towers." The saddle is often carved into ornate shapes, sometimes related to a particular totem or relationship that the maker may have, or had, with a supernatural or corporeal being. The saddle is generally made from wood, yet saddles have also been made from horn, bone, and metal. A rawhide saddle was noted in a museum piece, but that particular flute would not play. Either it was intended for display only, or the rawhide had totally lost its shape.

Though saddles are often cut from the same wood as the flute body, many contemporary flute makers use a wood that contrasts the color of the flute body, such

as a light colored wood (cedar) for the body, and a dark wood (walnut or mahogany) for the saddle. Regardless of the material used for the saddle, the tone is not affected. Bone or horn, being thick, allows the body of the flute to resonate more freely, but not significantly so.

After drawing the desired shape on a piece of 1/2" scrap wood, cut the saddle form using either a coping saw or band saw. Traditionalists should use a pocket knife and a "fork" of a tree limb. The saddle does not need to sit high, and it is best if it does not. If the saddle sits too high, it will catch on clothing or other loose items and is easily knocked out of place.

Various Saddle Shapes

The saddle does not sit tightly against the body of the flute, but rather needs a "u" shaped area or "chamfer" to direct the air forward and into the lower part of the body. The chamfer may either be carved into the saddle or made from cloth, cardboard, metal, or wood and glued to the body of the flute. It is very important that the chamfer be fairly close to the upper hole in order to prevent air from back flowing. The more accurate the airflow, the richer the tone of the flute.

Tie or rubber band together the two sections of the flute. It is not ready to be permanently glued at this time. Use a strip

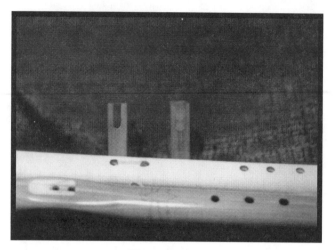

Chamfer Cut

of leather or rubber bands to attach the saddle over the holes and with the chamfer either carved into the saddle or in place on the flute body, blow into the mouthpiece. If all steps have been properly done, the flute will make its first sound!

The tone of the flute may be adjusted by moving the saddle forward or backward on the body, and once the "sweet spot," or best sounding area is found, lightly mark the position of the saddle on the body. This will allow the best tone of the flute to be found rapidly while drilling, carving, and tuning the finger holes.

Finger holes may be carved or drilled into the body by utilizing one of several methods; one traditional method is to place one's hands on the body of the flute while holding the mouthpiece against the lips. The places where the fingers naturally fall in two groups equidistant, are where the holes should be drilled. As the player's fingers curve on the body of the flute, so shall the holes not be drilled in a straight line. This method is more suited to the comfort of the player rather than having concern for tuning. Another traditional method is to measure using the palm of the hand placing the edge of the hand at the lower hole. The width of the hand determines the distance to the last or highest hole. The next lower hole is placed the distance of one knuckle below the highest hole. Each hole thereafter is measured in the same manner.

A more contemporary method is to carefully measure each hole based on the chosen length of the flute. The chart on Page 38 shows the length/hole measurement ratio for fairly accurate tuning.

It should be said here that the only reason for having any concern for tuning should be based on a desire to perform with tempered instruments such as guitar, piano, or synthesizers. The traditional flute is from nature, destined to speak to nature, with a natural emotion. The flute comes from a tree, and as two trees are not alike, neither are two flutes, even from the same tree. It is intended that the flute be an expression of the heart, therefore, regardless of how incorrect the tuning may be, the emotion put into the flute shall also come back out. With this in mind, unless a concert instrument is desired, the natural attitude of the wood, measured by nature's rulers, is that for which you should strive.

Once the holes have been drilled in their proper places, remove all of the rubber bands or leather ties. Lightly rub the edges of the two sections with either sandpaper, sandstone, or steel wool to remove finger oils. This will also further roughen the edges making for a better glue seal. Now the two sections are ready to be glued together, using either wood glue or hide glue (for the traditionalist). White glue is not good for this purpose, as it loosens with moisture and the flute may eventually come apart in places; particularly, in the upper chamber.

After the glue has had thirty-six to forty-eight hours to cure, the flute is ready to be finished. For a polished appearance, the flute body may be varnished taking care to not get the varnishing material inside the holes (plastic straws stuck in the holes will help here). For soft wood flutes, merely rubbing the wood with a light furniture oil is best. Varnish or polyurethane finishes will negatively affect the resonance of the wood. Another method to finish the wood is to "bone" it. Take a length of antler that has been rubbed smooth. A small piece of hardwood will work nearly as well. Rub the wood with a reasonable amount of pressure, moving rapidly back and forth,

creating heat combined with the friction. This will give the wood a glossy, and water resistant, finish. The harder the wood, the better this method works. Although boning is very time consuming, properly done, the finish is natural and does not negatively affect the tone. In woods of medium hardness, boning will actually brighten the tone.

Once the body has been finished to the makers goal, the same may be done with the saddle. Upon completion of the saddle, it may be attached to the body by using leather strips, or cotton cordage. Old flutes have been known to be tied with strips of cloth as well. Some flute makers

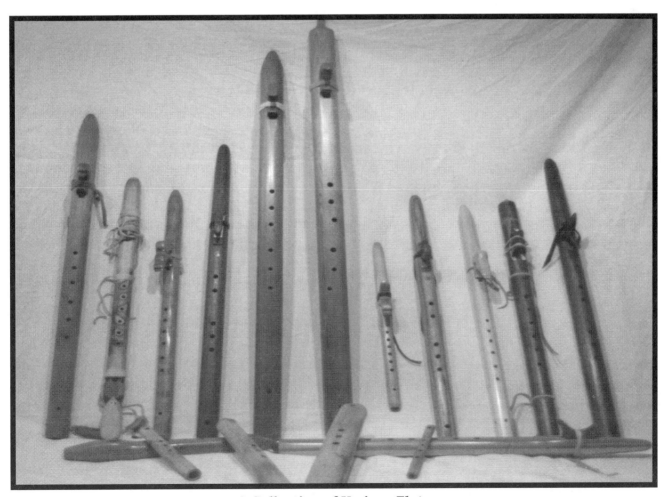

A Collection of Various Flutes

glue the saddle in place, yet this is not recommended. If the upper chamber should need to be cleaned, if humidity affects the tone of the flute, or if the chamfer swells or rots, then the saddle is difficult to remove if it has been glued.

The flute may be decorated in any number of methods; burning designs into the flute body with a wood pencil, paints either rubbed in or painted on, leather ties around the body, rawhide sewn wet onto the body, tied feathers, tied sage, sweetgrass, or cedar, carved designs or rings, or whatever imagination might create make for a personalized instrument. Traditional flutes had little decoration. The more decorated flutes in museums rarely can be played, while the plain flutes are more serviceable. Keep in mind that any decoration attached to the body of the flute, particularly decorations that encircle the body of the flute, will dampen the resonance of the flute walls.

Many of the older Plains flutes, particularly those of the Lakota, have bird heads and beaks carved into the bottom or end of the flute. Some Elders say that the crane is an erotic symbol. Among the Blackfeet, a white snow goose head carved into the end is commonly found.

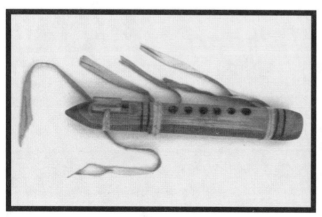

Southern Ute Juniper Flute

In any case, the goal is to create an instrument that sounds nice, evokes emotional expression, and is suitable to the maker, thereby making decoration secondary. No matter how beautiful the instrument may look, no pretty covering may compensate for poor tone.

SOUTHEASTERN CANE FLUTES

A length of cane is needed, preferably with no more than three septums or "breaks" throughout. The first cut is made midway between the upper septum and the middle septum, and the bottom cut is made immediately above the bottom septum, leaving a length of cane with only one septum. The septum or break should be located about three-quarters of the cane length. If a longer (lower pitch) flute is desired, the septum sections may be removed by careful burning with a hot rod, by drilling with a long drill bit, or by waiting until the finger holes are drilled and removing the septum with a crafting knife.

Two holes are drilled, one on each side of the remaining septum. The holes should be of equal diameter. The hole below the septum, nearest the end or bottom of the flute, should be lightly filed at an angle to the inside of the cane. This will thin out the lower edge of the hole, allowing air to be split between the inner and outer sections of the flute. By cutting a flat channel over the two holes, the angle into the lower body is more readily accomplished. A small chamfer is cut over the septum, which will allow for free air flow once the flute is complete, and the saddle in place.

Finger holes must be drilled in the lower body of the cane, using either a 3/8"

A Traditional Yuma Cane Flute

35

drill bit or a hot length of metal of similar diameter. The first hole, nearest the mouthpiece, should be drilled approximately four fingers, or three and a half inches, below the angled hole. Each of the following holes should be drilled one finger, or 3/4 of an inch, apart. The number of holes in the Southeastern flutes varies from 4 to 6 holes.

After the holes are drilled the downward edges are beveled. This not only allows for a tight fit beneath the finger, it helps prevent the cane from splintering. Once the holes are beveled, all cuts and holes should be burned with an iron or candle flame.

A saddle is required, just as with the Plains style flutes. The saddle should be the same width as the flattened area above the two air passage holes. As there is already a chamfer in place above the septum, no chamfer is required. Simply tie

the saddle in place, adjust back and forth until the optimum tone is found, tie the saddle thong tightly, and the flute is complete.

FLUTE MAINTENANCE

All flutes require maintenance, just as any instrument, fine furniture, or any other object of quality. Although the effort needed is minimal, it is necessary in order to maintain the quality of the instruments sound. It also affords the flute owner an opportunity to become more familiar with the workings of the flute, and to experiment with different positions of the saddle for tone and tuning.

Playing the flute for any length of time generates moisture inside the upper cham-

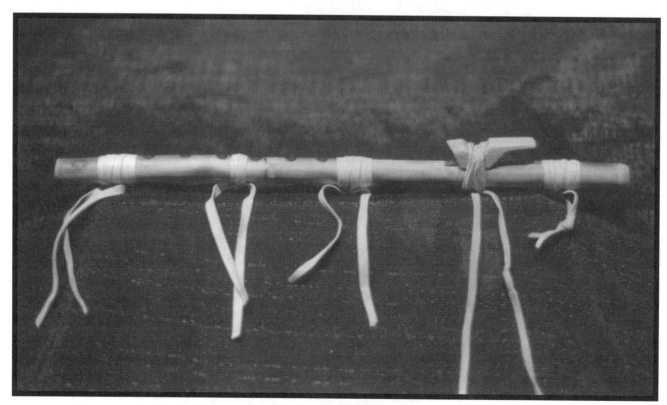

Example of a South Eastern Cane Flute

ber, and under the saddle. A small amount of moisture will also be found in the lower chamber. With this in mind, after each playing session with the flute, the user should hold the flute by the lower section, swinging the upper chamber towards the ground, rapidly shaking excess moisture out of the upper chamber. With flutes that have removeable saddles, the saddle should be removed, and the deck upon which it sits should be wiped down and dried. If this effort to keep the upper chamber dry is not consistent, then the flute owner runs a risk of having the upper chamber either warp, splitting the seam where the two halves of the body join. This may cause the block to eventually crack, allowing upper chamber air to leak into the lower chamber. In any case, this is not healthy for the flute.

Periodically, oil should be poured into the upper portion of the flute and allowed to sit for a few minutes before pouring the oil back out. A high grade furniture oil will suffice. Under no circumstances should a food grade or aromatic oil be used, as this will encourage the growth of bacteria, which is not good for the player nor for the flute. Corn, vegetable, soybean, and other natural oils should not be used. Formby's™ Old English™ or other furniture grade oils are good choices.

The outer areas of the flute should also be rubbed with this same oil, allowing the wood pores to accept the oil, with any excess wiped off. This protects all areas of the wood.

Hardwood flutes are by far easier to maintain. They do not readily absorb moisture, and they take bumps and knocks quite well. They do need to be cared for in nearly the same manner as a softwood flute, particularly with regard to oiling the body every 6 months or so. The frequency of maintenance is dependent entirely upon the geographical area in which the flute resides. Humid and hot climates call for more regular maintenance, particularly in terms of making sure that the upper chamber is dry each time the flute is put away following every use. Dry climates necessitate regular oilings, but do not require as much effort with regards to keeping the upper chamber dry.

The flute should be kept in a case of some kind, protecting it from bumps, scratches during transport, and curious animals. If the flute body or saddle is tied with leather or rawhide, insects and animals will find the instrument a tasty treat. Buckskin sewn into a long bag is most common, or even simply wrapping a piece of leather around the entire flute works as well. A bit of old blanket will also suffice. Hard cases may be made from a large diameter length of PVC pipe, or cardboard tubing similar to that which is found in the center of a roll of carpet. One flute manufacturer offers a case of buckskin that has several PVC tubes in it capable of carrying 5 or more flutes. It closely resembles a golf bag, cut down to a shorter size, with shoulder straps for backpacking.

Should the flute be a wood easily discolored from moist fingers, body oils, or simply seems to attract dirt that will not wipe off, the entire body of the flute may be gently rubbed with OOO grade steel wool. Remove the saddle from the body, and

evenly apply the steel wool to the entire body. In soft wood flutes with severe dirt or oil, this effort will actually brighten the overall sound of the flute in most cases. It will also give the flute a brand new appearance.

Lastly, remember always that the flute is an extension of the person playing it. The flute will not play properly if the owner does not respect it; without care you will never bring forth the emotions contained within either the instrument nor the owner. This instrument is born from a living being, a tree, and therefore should be respected as any other thing on this earth.

Overall length of flute/inside diameter	Bottom of flute to bottom finger hole	Bottom (fifth) hole to fourth finger hole	Fourth hole to third finger hole	Third hole to second finger hole	Second hole to first finger hole	First finger hole to lowest chamber hole	Mouth piece to highest chamber hole	Makes a flute in the key of:
27 1/2" 1"	7 1/4"	1 1/8"	1 1/8"	2 15/16"	1 1/8"	4 1/4"	8 5/8"	E minor G major
23 1/4" 7/8"	5 1/2"	1 1/8"	1 1/4"	2 1/16"	1"	3 7/8"	7 1/2"	A minor C major
19 3/4" 5/8"	4 3/4"	1 3/8"	1 3/8"	2 9/16"	1 1/8"	4 1/8"	4 1/8"	F# minor D major

Demonstrating the Length/Hole Measurement Ratio

MAKING A NATIVE AMERICAN FLUTE

(Author's Note: While descriptions, in general terms, of the components of flutes may be found in the preceeding chapter, this section is specific to the construction of a Native American Flute and includes step-by-step instructions and pictures to do so.)

Begin with two pieces of 1 inch x 2 inch white pine stock, matched in a length between 18 and 26 inches in length. Try to avoid wood with large knots, as it will be difficult to work around them. Draw a pattern on the wood, marking the area to be cut out, leaving approximately 1/4 inch of wood on the sides of the cut and leaving an uncut area near the top of the wood pieces (see photo). This uncut area will join the top and bottom of the flute pieces, creating

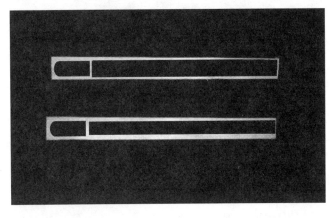

an airtight chamber, where the air passing through the flute is controlled. It is very important that these two pieces of wood not be disturbed during the next process. Also try to draw the lines within a quarter of an inch or less from the outside edge of the wood.

The more thin the walls of the flute are, the more clear and bright the flute will be. Vibration is the key to a solid flute sound and the greater the mass, the less vibration. Using either a router or chisel, (for the first time flute maker a router is fastest, cleanest, and easiest to use) begin to clean out the wood area covered by the drawn template. Again, be sure not to damage the "bridge" area where the two chambers are closed off. Also take special care not to cut so deep that the wood is thinner

than 1/16 of an inch at any point. Although thin wood makes for a wonderful sound, wood that is cut through to the other side makes no sound at all. For the first time flute maker, it is best to err on the side of caution.

Once the two halves are equally carved out, and the wall thickness is consistent all the way down the chamber length, move on to the next step.

Putting aside one of the two pieces of wood, use a 3/8 drill bit, drill a hole on each side of the "bridge" section of the flute, **on one half only!** This piece of the flute body will be the topside of the flute. Be sure the the hole on the shorter side of the bridge is straight up and down with no angle. The hole on the lower side may be angled slightly, as this hole

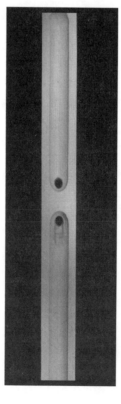

also needs to be filed at the lower portion so as to remove the "roundness" of the hole. This angle better directs the airflow into the lower chamber and keeps the airflow from being obstructed in it's movement. Be sure that the angle 'ramps' the air into the lower chamber. It is this step in the flute making process that will determine the breathiness or solidness of the flute's sound. If the angle is too sharp, (45 degrees or more) the sound will be very breathy and lacking in solid tone. If the ramp is too thin, the flute will be squeaky and have little control. Unfortunately, there is no formula for developing the exact angle, as each piece of wood is different from another. Even two flutes created from the same wood stock will have different sounds. If there is any trepidation in making the angle correct, move on to the next step, and come back to the angle at a later time.

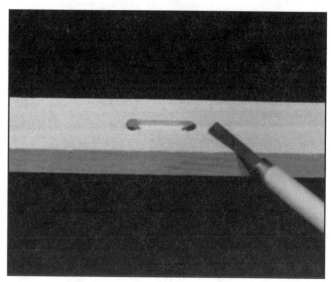

Using a small wood chisel, cut a straight chamfer or "cutout" between the two holes in the top of the flute body. These two holes, plus the chamfer, are the directing forces on the air entering and exiting the flute chambers. The area should be approximately 1/16 of an inch in depth and

1/8 to 3/16 of an inch wide. Again, too much depth or width will make the flute sound breathy and without solid tone. If a breathy, mystical sound is desired, experiment with depths and widths of the chamfer.

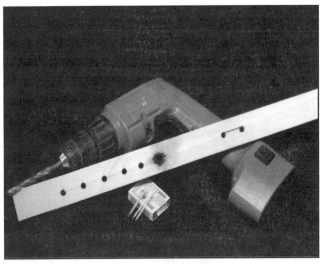

Measuring from the lower hole of the flute body (the hole furthest from what will become the mouthpiece) mark a line that is 4 inches below the lower edge of the hole. This shall become the first finger hole of the flute. Now measure the next hole 1 and 1/2 inches below the first marking. This becomes the second finger hole. The remainder of the finger hole markings should be 1 and 1/4 inch apart from each other. Make sure that the markings are exactly in the center of the flute body. Make a cross line over each marking so that *X* marks the spot.

With a 3/8 or a 1/4 inch drill bit, drill each finger hole slowly, without too much pressure, so as not to split the wood. The beginning craftsman may wish to place masking tape over both sides of the wood to help prevent the drill bit from wandering and/or splitting the wood. Remember, the chamber walls are very thin and will

not withstand much pressure.

After the holes are drilled, (remove any tape that may have been placed on the flute body) use a candle, lighter, or even a match, to lightly burn the edges of the holes on the outside of the flute body. Doing so will help prevent the wood from "fingering" or fraying up during the next processes. If the wood frays or, in other words, develops small hairs or splinters while sanding and finishing, it makes a good finger seal more difficult to obtain when playing the finished flute.

Once the holes are lightly burned, the two halves are ready to be joined together. Wood glue, placed on all edges of the flute body, with extra care taken to thoroughly cover both halves of the bridge sections, will create an airtight space. This is critical, as air leaks cause the flute to have a very poor sound, if it allows for any sound at all.

Immediately place the two halves together. Be sure that the edges line up correctly, and the lengths line up correctly before leaving the glue to dry. If they do not line up correctly, then the chamber cannot vibrate evenly, not to mention that there is a high risk of a leaky area. Use

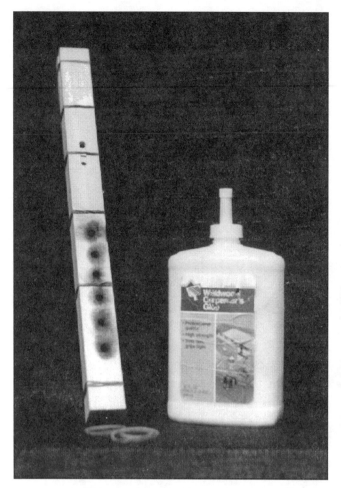

Shake out any sawdust that may have accumulated in the upper chamber. This sawdust should easily be shaken out of the upper chamber hole in the top side of the flute. Once the majority of the sawdust is shaken out, blow into the mouthpiece, and the rest of the sawdust will most likely be forced out of the upper chamber via the upper hole. Make sure that safety goggles are worn at this step to prevent the sawdust from getting in the eyes!!

several rubber bands to hold the halves in place and allow the flute to dry for at least twenty-four hours, or longer, depending on the manufacturer's recommended glue drying times.

Remove the rubber bands. Now look at the end of the flute that will become the mouthpiece. The glue joint makes a line at exactly the one-half point of the end. Draw a line perpendicular to the glue line that is exactly in the middle of the two outside edges of the flute body. Using a 1/8 or 3/16 inch drill bit, carefully drill a straight hole into the end of the flute body, until the end of the drill bit reaches the carved out area of the upper chamber. This is where the air is blown into the flute. You may want to lightly burn this hole as well.

Using sand paper and a knife, begin to work the body of the flute into a round shape. An experienced woodworker should be able to use a router for this function. The more round the flute is, the thinner the walls become, again creating the wonderful, haunting sound for which the flute is so well known. Take extra caution to be sure that the wood is not cut through to the inside area or all the work up to this point is for naught and the only thing achieved is a fine piece of firewood.

Once the body has achieved a fairly rounded form, round off the mouthpiece end of the flute until it feels comfortable between the lips. This area will be a constant irritation if it is not carved and sanded

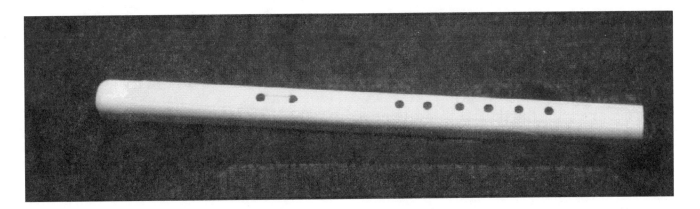

to a comfortable, smooth finish. For a beginner, an end that resembles the end of a broom handle is desirable. Use sand paper to complete the finish work on the body, making sure that it is smooth and without any frayed or rough spots. This step is important, as it determines the absolute final shape of the flute body and it must be light, balanced and comfortable to hold in the mouth and hand. If it is not so, then the instrument will be doomed to the mantlepiece for show rather than use.

The final appearance of the flute body should be similar to the photo at the top of this page.

Now a saddle is needed to direct the air exiting from the upper chamber into the lower chamber. This is accomplished by making a saddle, also known as a *bird*, or *block*. The saddle may be elaborately carved or simply a flat piece of wood. Either works equally well as this is a utilitarian function.

The saddle (shown to the right) is easy to make with a pocketknife and sand paper, using a bit of scrap wood left over from the body-making process. The only necessary measurements are that the saddle be perfectly flat on one side and that the saddle be wide enough to cover the chamfer carved between the two upper holes in the flute body. The length and height of the saddle

have no real bearing on the direction of air.

Test the saddle by holding it tightly over the two holes on the upper body of the flute. The saddle should just reach the upper edge of the lower hole, so that all of the lower hole is visible. The upper hole should be completely covered, so that no air may escape from the top or sides of the saddle/body joint. If the saddle is properly flat and the area over the two holes is sufficiently flat, then the flute should make it's first noise at this point. If not, then don't worry as there are still several things that may need to be corrected.

First, check the angle of the wood where the air enters the lower chamber. Is it ramped into the lower chamber at an angle of less than 45 degrees? Is it thin and sharp at the lower portion of the hole as it should be? If not, now is the time to

correct it. If the angle does not thin out properly, then the air is being obstructed where it is to flow into the lower chamber.

File a little bit, then replace the saddle, and test again. This process may take several re-visits with the file. Go slowly, as it is easy to remove wood and very difficult to replace wood. Patience is well exercised here.

Once a solid sound is heard, stop filing immediately. The rest of the notes must be checked and once a solid timbre is achieved, several alternatives to improving sound are available.

Using a piece of leather long enough to go around the body of the flute at least two times, tie the saddle tightly in place. Now check the tone of all of the notes by covering all six holes and blowing into the mouthpiece. Blow gently, with increasing pressure, until a desireable tone is heard. Now, remove the fingers from one hole at a time, carefully listening for changes in the

tone and not the pitch of the flute. Pitch is related to the distance between finger holes; tone is related to air flow. If the notes all have an equal tone, then move onto the next step. If the tone is inconsistent, then try moving the saddle back and forth between the holes with very small incremental movements. A little move goes a long way in changing pitch.

If the desired tone cannot be reached by moving the saddle up and down the body, then the angle of the lower hole in the upper chamber must be re-examined. This assumes that there are no air leaks anywhere in the body of the flute. This angle should be sharp, with no curve in the slope as it enters the lower chamber. It should be sufficiently thin as to "split" the air exiting the saddle/chamfer area.

At this point, assuming that all notes have an equal, or near equal, timbre or tone, the flute may be considered completed but for finishing. Finish work may be elabo-

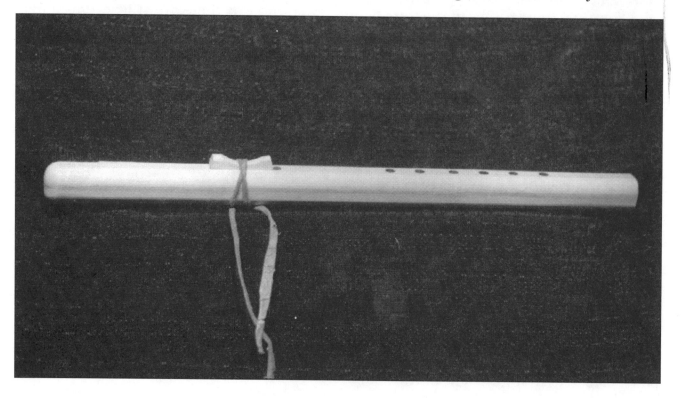

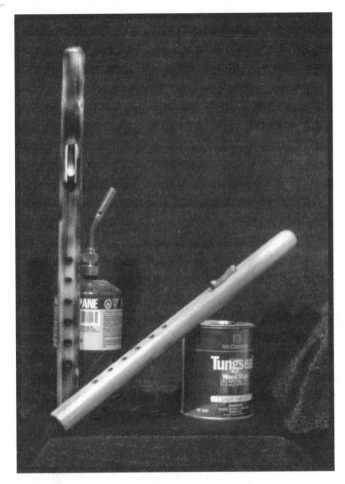

rate, or very simple. Oiling the wood may be sufficient or using a varnish may be a chosen finish material. Keep in mind, an increase in the mass or thickness of the lower chamber walls will result in loss of tone.

One alternative to varnish or shellac is to use a propane torch and lightly "burn" the wood to create a smooth finished ap-

pearance. After the wood is burned, it may be rubbed to remove any soot and a high quality furniture wax or polish may be deeply rubbed on the body. Or, a fine oil stain might be all that is wanted.

When finishing, it is best to remove the saddle from the body, unless the saddle is to be permanently glued in place. It is not desirable to glue the saddle, unless the maker decides that the tone of the flute is perfect and does not want the future option of working with the overall tone and quality of sound. For most purposes, attaching the saddle with a leather thong is best. Should the flute change over time, having the saddle "removable" is an important option, not to mention making it much easier to clear insects or other material that may find their way into the upper chamber.

The flute is now complete! Take care of it, respect it and be proud of the creation, both musical and functional. A light re-oiling every year or so and taking care to clear the upper chamber of moisture after playing for a length of time, are all that should be needed to maintain the instrument for many years. After the first flute is made, take the knowledge gained and move on to the next one and make it even better. It may take several attempts before creating the *Stradivarius* of flutes, but think of the wonderful collection you'll have. Experiment and have fun!!

NOTES

FLUTE PLAYING TECHNIQUES

Playing the Native American flute is not as difficult as the making of one. Making sound come out of a hollow stick requires only two things; breath and emotion. If the player can breathe emotion into the stick, the wood will interpret the emotional input and transform it into beautiful music. The best way that I have ever described my role in playing on the flute is that *the player becomes the vessel which holds water, but not the water itself. Nor is the player the one that puts water in the vessel and shall not be the one to pour the water out. The player merely holds the water and puts his own temporary shape to the water.*

Each flute, having come from a living human being (a tree), has it's own unique voice and it is the responsibility of the player/maker to find and understand the limitations and values of that voice. And, during the discovery of the personality of the flute, the player will develop a relationship with that flute enabling him or her to better express emotion and thought.

The flute, being "end blown" with four to six holes, is from a classification of wind blown instruments known as *flute-a-bec*. When air is blown into the end of the flute, it collects pressure in the first chamber, passes through the chamfer and, directed by the saddle, enters the second chamber. In this way, the notes are generated by "lengthening or shortening" the over-all flute by finger placement over the various holes. All aspects of the flutes' manufac-

ture relate to pitch, tone and ease of play. The bore size affects both pitch and timbre; the width of the flute walls affect timbre and apparent pitch; the saddle and chamfer assembly control the amount of wind or breath needed to make the flute function properly and in pitch; and, the length of the overall flute is the primary determining factor in the pitch/key of the flute. By changing any of these factors, the flute will play, sound and breathe differently.

The scale of the instrument is related to the length of the instrument, yet primarily regulated by the spacing of the finger holes. The majority of commercially available flutes tend to fall into the musical key classifications of between F# minor to A minor. There are many key signatures available and they range from a low G minor, below middle C, to a high G minor an octave above G/middle C. Pitch is not a significant consideration, however, unless the player's intention is to perform on the flute with an orchestra or band. If this is the case, then the player must be aware that the Native flute is not evenly tempered across it's own scale. Pitches must be "blown in." In other words, the amount of breath used to create the tone will need to be increased or decreased to achieve the desired pitch. This is particularly true in the lowest and highest notes of the scale. Keep in mind that this lack of even temper is one of the factors making the Native flute

such a haunting, soothing instrument. Because our brain registers the instrument as being slightly off pitch from the "normal" sounds associated with most music, it appeals to the emotional senses more so than the mental. It also allows the flute to create tones not found in standard or modern tunings and allows the player to generate phrasing not possible with standard instruments.

To play the flute, first grasp the flute loosely by covering the upper two or three holes of the flute with the left hand, beginning with the index finger at the top of the holes, and the middle and ring fingers subsequently covering the lower hole(s). The right hand then covers the lower 3 holes, with the index finger covering the upper hole, the middle finger covering the middle hole, and the ring finger covering the lowest hole.

Place the end of the flute in the mouth,

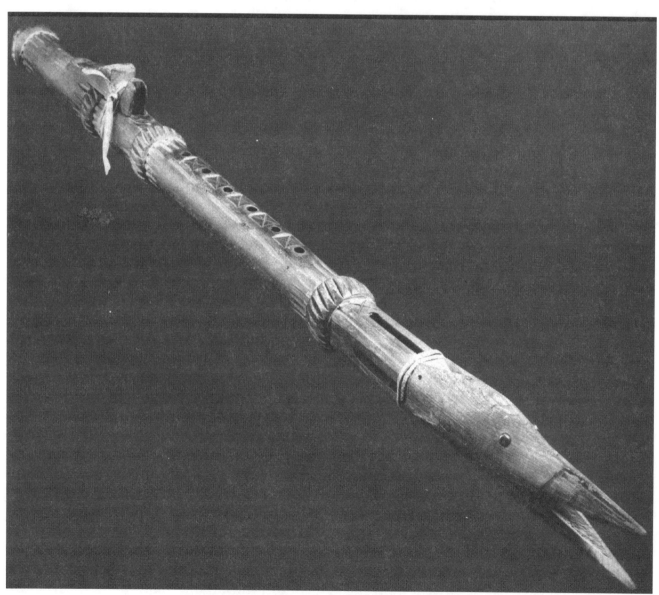

Traditional Lakota Flute from the mid 1800s

A Sketch done by George Catlin
Notice the Flute and War Club

The Proper Way to Hold the Flute

again, pressing lightly. At no point should the player need to use heavy pressure!!! Gently breathe air into the flute, while covering all finger holes. Continue to blow air until a solid, strong fundamental tone is heard. Once that tone is found, breathe air into the flute maintaining a steady tone. Insure that the tone does not rise or fall in either pitch or timbre. Practice maintaining this sound until it is possible to achieve proper pitch even after taking a breath. It is important at this point that proper breathing skills are achieved or the player will not be able to create certain sounds or techniques mentioned later on in this section. Do not be intimidated or frustrated if at first achieving the correct breathing doesn't come immediately. It takes time, practice and a developed relationship with the flute in order to obtain this skill. Once a pleasing tone is developed, everything else will seem to fall into place.

One trick I have used to help players that seem to have a difficult time getting to the point where their breathing seems to stabilize, is to have them play the flute via their nose. This is how the Hawaiians play their flutes, with the exception that the Hawaiians cover one nostril while using the other to breathe wind into the flute. (This practice stems from the Polynesian belief that as the mouth may be used to say evil things, the nose breath is more pure because the nose cannot speak. Therefore, the music that comes from the nose blown flute is more pure than that of a mouth blown flute.)

Place the mouthpiece of the flute against one nostril. Breathe out of the nose while covering the finger holes as they would normally be covered. Develop a tone in the same manner as mentioned above. Once the desired tone is achieved, then the flute may be wiped and played from the mouth. Simply remember the lung inflation/deflation rate at which the flute best played while being blown from the nostril. While this may sound silly, and look strange, this method helps many people develop the proper outflow or breathing techniques required to generate the mellow, mature tones for which the Native flute is so well known.

Assuming that the player is able to generate the desired tone continuously, finger movement becomes the next step in learning the flute. Begin by first blowing the continuous fundamental note with all finger holes covered. While continuing the air flow, lift the ring finger from the lowest hole. The speed at which this finger leaves the hole will determine the accuracy of the arrival of the new note. Practice lifting this finger from the flute until the new note is heard cleanly and clearly, with little or no bend. If the note seems to "crack" or squeal

when the finger is first lifted, this indicates that there is too much air pressure behind the note. Therefore, lessen the amount of breath going into the flute when removing the finger. Learning to breath more powerfully or less powerfully when moving fingers is another very important technique to use with the flute. This will come in very handy when practicing other playing styles mentioned later in this section.

Practice this technique until all holes may be uncovered in sequence, beginning with the lowest hole and working to the uppermost hole; maintain an even balance in pitch change, timbre change and volume. The sequence is generally that no lower holes are covered, with upper holes uncovered, unless the player is attempting to "overblow" the note. That is, creating notes in the upper scale. As the player moves up the scale, it will be noted that breath control and increased pressure are necessary.

Noting that the scale shown below indicates notes beyond the five or six holes currently being uncovered, the player now moves into the realm of "overblown notes." These notes are blown with greater pressure, while covering the lowermost two, and next adjacent holes on the flute (see illustration below for correct scale/covering). The scale changes in timbre during these overblown notes and this is to be expected and accepted. After all, nearly twice the amount of pressure is generated for the higher overblown notes than is used to create the lower, less aggressive tones.

By learning these overblown notes, the scale of the flute is extended by two to three notes. This makes the flute more accessible to moving melody. Further, a greater scale makes expression a more expansive and personal representation.

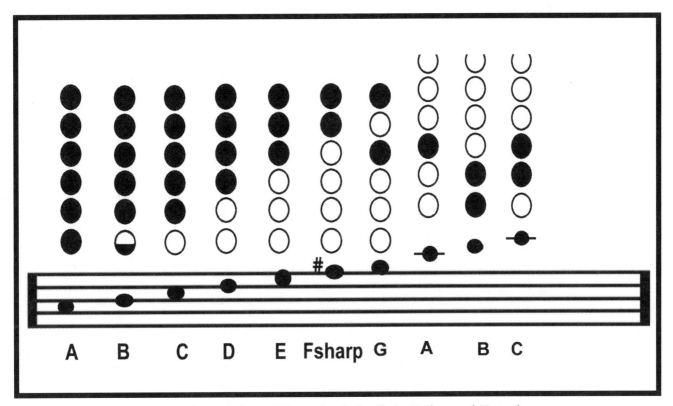

Illustration of the A Minor Scale both in Holes and Notations

After these fundamental scale movements are smooth and squeak free, the player should have a good grasp of what the flute will do at various pitch points. Now the player may move on to other techniques that will make the sound of the flute a unique posession; one matched by no other person. This sonic *signature* is what separates the various flute players from one another and allows each player their own distinctive expression of emotion and statement.

Breathing skills and diaphragm control are two of the most important factors in being able to create some of the more difficult sounds heard from the greatest flute players. Being able to properly manipulate the tongue is another important skill, as tonguing, combined with accurate breathing, is what entirely controls the flute timbre and expression.

Begin practicing breathing by first starting a light breath that grows in intensity while holding a fundamental note. Do this with all holes covered. Observe that the note seems to "bend" into place. This bend or *glissando* may be further enhanced by slightly lifting the finger off of the hole as the pressure increases. Doing so will actually take the flute to the next note, or step, in pitch and makes a beautiful haunting sound when done correctly. This technique may be applied to any note on the flute. Bends are easily accomplished, yet getting a bend to appear smooth and seamless takes a great deal of practice. A useful tip regarding glissando in the upper notes

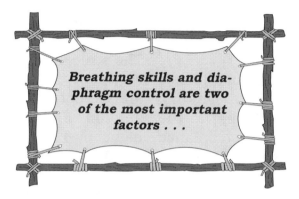

Breathing skills and diaphragm control are two of the most important factors . . .

is to be sure to lessen the pressure just **before** the note is bent, or the fingers are lifted. Trying to start a bend in the middle of a phrase without lessening the pressure, simply sounds like a bend with no expression and will often squeak or squeal in the movement. This happens when the air is temporarily displaced if there is no change in the pressure behind the note.

This technique may also be applied to downward bending notes as well. Simply lessen the pitch just prior to the fingers being applied to the hole and be sure that the finger arrives at the hole with equal timing. Insure that the finger firmly seats over the hole once the pitch is bent to it's lowest possible point.

Another signature sound that seems to be associated with most flute players is a "bark" or stopped sound. This sound may be achieved with either breathing or more commonly, tonguing.

As the note is being blown, the tongue is pressed hard against the back of the teeth, or "slammed". This stops the air flow to the flute very quickly and makes the note die immediately. The note may also be started the same way, with the tongue against the teeth and released from the teeth very rapidly, making the note seem to be very aggressive. This technique is very useful in playing *staccato* passages.

If a rapid bend or finger movement accompanies the tongue slam, the note will bark or bite. This technique is often used to change phrases in the song, or to punctuate a particular passage. The manner in

which this technique is used is employed by several well known flute artists in order to better define and individualize their personal sound.

Tonguing effects are also used in other styles, one of which is to flutter the tongue against the top of the mouth, creating a vibration that manifests its sound as a *staccato vibrato* that sounds much like an old fashion alarm clock.

To best practice this technique, put the flute down and form the lips into an "O" shape. With the tongue relaxed and flat against the bottom of the mouth, use medium pressure to blow air out through the lips. Loosely lift the tongue while blowing air out and the tongue will naturally begin to vibrate. If the tongue is not loose and relaxed, it will not vibrate. Picture a flag blowing in a high wind and the way it sounds as the wind flows around it. The sound generated from the tongue vibration

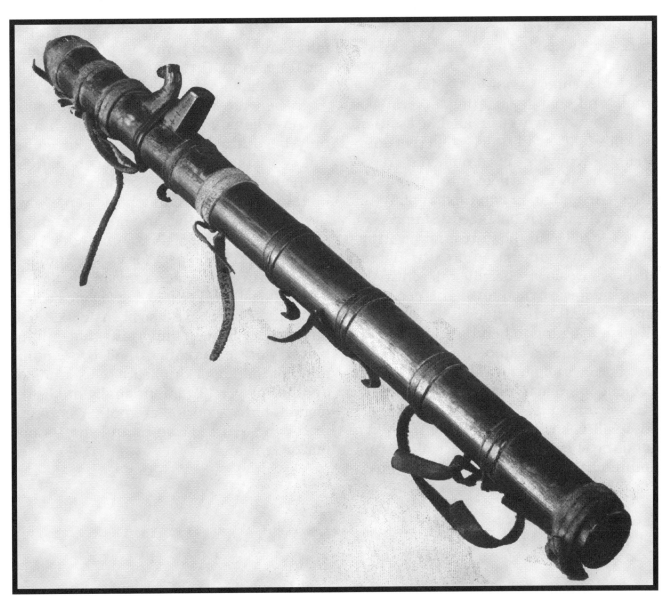

Traditional Fox Flute

should sound similar. Too much pressure will be messy causing the tongue to tighten up and making the lips feel numb. Therefore, be sure that only enough pressure required to cause the tongue to begin to vibrate is used. Once the tongue is in the correct motion, little is required to continue the effect.

Now pick up the flute and practice creating this sound with the flute and the tongue. If too much pressure is used, the flute will merely squeak and scream. Learn to maintain even pressure in the same manner as when the fundamental tone was learned.

By learning to vibrate the tongue, stop a note and change fingering, several wonderful sounds may be created. *Glissandos* or bends take on an entirely different sound when these styles are combined.

Overblowing a note into pitch is another effect that is achieved rapidly and easily if the flute is balanced. Simply cover all of the holes in the flute and, beginning with a slow evenly paced breath, increase the pressure flow. The note will gently slide from the lowest note to the higher octave note. While this technique is easily accomplished, learning to bend an octave in the lower three notes can be frustrating.

The overall quality of the flute plays a tremendous role in the class of sound that the instrument may produce. A thin walled flute will easily slip out of control in the hands of a beginner yet will permit for rapid timbre changes and bright tongue effects

that a similar sized flute of thicker walls might not allow. Hardwood flutes are not as easily manipulated as a softwood flute, such as one made of cedar or white pine.

Finger hole angles, upper chamber length, saddle height and key signature of the flute will also play a role in what sounds the flute may generate. Therefore, do not be frustrated nor disappointed if one particular flute does not allow the player to create the same sounds as one heard in a recording or a sound heard in the head. Either accept the lack of availability of specific sounds or continue to practice making flutes until the desired tone, key or effect is created and heard.

There are dozens of similar techniques to those listed above, many of which may only be utilized with any one particular flute. Just as some horses may be taught particular tricks that other horses cannot be taught, flutes are much the same way. It would be rare that any one flute might show the player all of the sounds contained therein. Out of respect for various professional flute players, many professional techniques that have been developed on an individual basis have also been deliberately omitted. It is very important that a flute player work on creating their own sound and not imitate or duplicate the sounds of another player. To intentionally duplicate or imitate the sounds of another is to attempt to steal their voice and that is not fair or ethical.

DRUMS

In the earliest of times, drums were used to accompany songs, to communicate and to represent the heartbeat of the earth. The first drum was most likely nothing more than stomping on the earth. At some later point drummers would stretch a hide between themselves, holding on to the hide with one hand and using either their hands or a stick in the other. Even later, the concept of staking a hide over a hole in the ground came about and the construction of drums, in some form, became a regular event. Hollowed logs soon followed and built up frames were not far behind.

The drums used in indigenous music come in a huge variety of sizes, styles and forms. Drum frames may be made from elaborately joined pieces of wood, carved out tree trunks, old drum shells from a trap kit, beauty rims from a wheel and almost anything else that the hide can be stretched over.

Drum heads might be made out of commercially tanned cow, elk, horse or deer hides, but are most commonly covered by rawhide. Rawhide lasts for a long time and

A Comparison of Traditional (left) and Contemporary Pow Wow Drums

1832 Sketch by George Catlin of White Buffalo (Blackfoot) with his Medicine Drum

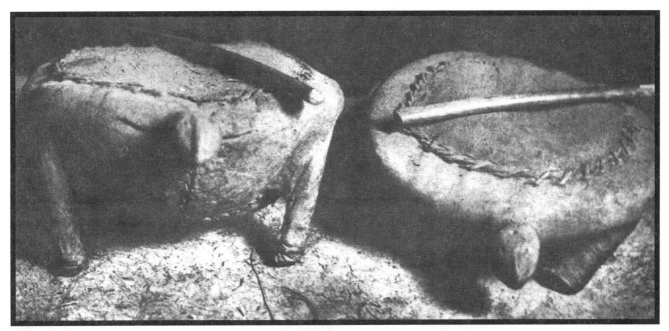

Edward Curtis nearly paid for this photograph with his life. Although he underwent a sweat ceremony with the keeper of the turtle drums, and paid several hundred dollars to photograph these spiritual implements, several members of the House of the Turtle were not in agreement with the Keeper of the Turtles. Twenty five members chased Curtis and his Assiniboine associates from the area after he photographed these drums. Each of these drums holds the spirit of a buffalo and, thus, are very heavy. This is the only known photograph of these instruments and, as they are not objects to be reproduced, no measurements, materials or methods of construction are described herein.

may be put on while wet, shrinking and rising in pitch as it dries. Some drums have one head, or covering, others have two heads, while some drums are made from forked trees, giving them three heads.

If you wish to make your own drum, frames may be manufactured or obtained in many ways. There are companies that specialize in manufacturing premade drum frames, ranging from four inch diameter to forty inches in diameter and from one inch in depth to twenty inches in depth. These frames may be purchased at either music stores, that carry standard drums, or purchased from most Native American crafting suppliers. Once in a while, an old drum set or single drum can be found at a ga-

rage sale or flea market. Remove the head and hardware and a perfect frame is obtained for a very low price. Many craft supply stores also have compressed wood rings used for home decorating that, although very heavy, are often suitable.

A fallen tree that is of the desired diameter is the traditional way of making drums. Soft woods are best for beginners. Woods such as pine, cottonwood, cedar, spruce, Chinese elm and willow are very easily obtained in quantity and are soft enough for learning how to hollow out a drum frame. Walnut, birch, mahogany and ash are great woods for a drum frame, albeit that they make a very heavy frame and are much harder to work with hand tools.

A section is cut out of the fallen tree that is of the determined depth and width of the drum. Then the log is hollowed out starting from the middle and working out to the sides. The bark must be removed and the sides of the drum should not exceed one inch in thickness. If the drum frame is too thick, the drum will not resonate properly. The thinner the finished drum shell, the more resonant and "big"

the sound of the completed drum shall be. Just be careful not to make the frame so thin that it cannot support the tension of the rawhide head. Only fallen trees should be used, preferably from trees that have been laying for a year or more. Drum frames cut from fresh or newly felled trees will not cure correctly, causing the frame to either warp or crack under the stress of the drum head. It is very important that

From a photograph taken by Curtis in 1908, this tambourine-style drum has a head made from the stomach of a walrus and is used primarily in winter. These drums vary in diameter from one to five feet. The one pictured above measures forty-two inches. The drum moves from horizontal to vertical when being played and the drumstick is a slender wand.

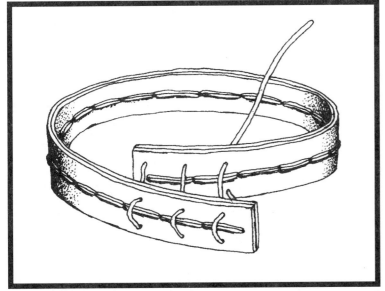

When the two ends are tied together, this Drum Frame will be Constructed from a Reservation Cheese Box

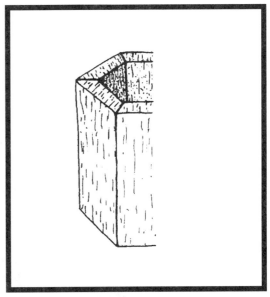

Using 1" x 4" Wood Lengths, a Drum Frame may be Constructed

the wood be dry and air dried wood is always best. Soft woods such as cottonwood or pine make very bright sounding and lightweight drums.

If the drum is to be one-sided (that is, with only one head), then holes should be drilled in the frame for rawhide stays which will hold the single head in place. For a two sided drum, the stays or laces will be shared by both heads.

Another method of creating drum frames is to use 1" x 4" or 1" x 6" pieces of

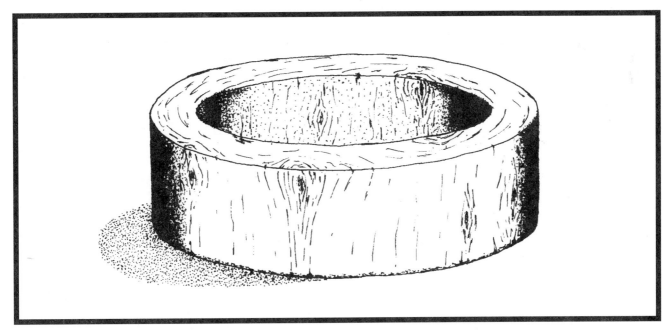

This Drum Frame has been Constructed from an Old, Dry Log

wood of a length cut to the depth of the drums final size. The edges of the wood are beveled on each side and then glued together. The diameter of the drum will determine the number of wood pieces required.

Woodworkers "biscuits" are also good for holding the frame together. Cowhide is particularly strong and will bend all but the strongest of frames. As with the traditional style drum, a one-headed drum will need holes drilled in the frame to hold the single head. A two head drum will share the stays or laces with the opposite head.

Beauty rims from various cars will work for a drum frame, as will a cheese box, 55 gallon container or nearly any open round object; however, the primary purpose of the drum is to connect with the earth or to at least represent the earth.

Collection of Hand Drums (NAC Water Drum at Bottom)

Therefore, natural materials should be used whenever possible.

Once the frame has been built or obtained, it must be covered. Rawhide is the best material for this from a traditional and practical view and may be obtained from any tannery, craft supply, or leather outlet. It can also easily be made at home.

For smaller, hand-held drums, rawhide from deer, elk or goat are most desirable. The thinner rawhide is easier to work with and offers a "sweeter" sound. Small drums made from thick rawhide sound dull and lifeless; they also have little or no "pitch." Larger drums require cow, horse or elk hide, both from a perspective of size and strength.

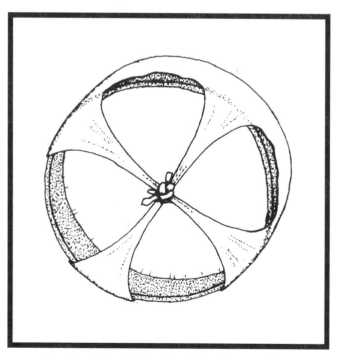

Soaked Rawhide Stretched over the Drum Frame

Lacing Techniques used on Hand Drums pictured on Page 60

The rawhide should be soaked until loose and pliable. Larger hides that are thick must be soaked overnight. Warm, not hot, water speeds the process somewhat, but keep in mind that hot water can "burn" or ruin the hide. Once the hide is pliable, it may be cut to fit the drum frame.

Place the frame on the outstretched rawhide and, with a pencil, trace the outline of the drum. Add at least one inch of extra diameter for stretch over the frame and to attach the thongs or pins to hold the head in place. If the drum is to be covered on both ends, trace each end individually. If the head is to be held in place with thongs, punch holes in the rawhide at least two inches apart. Match the spacing and number of holes on the opposite head.

The extra rawhide left over should be cut in a continuous strip or thong, which will be used to hold the head to the frame. While cutting the thong, it may be best to put the newly cut heads back in water, so that it will re-soften.

Place the wet rawhide head on the frame with all sides of the rawhide hanging over the frame being equal. Use thumbtacks or upholstery tacks to loosely hold the head in place. Stretch the head tightly over the frame as tacks are put into place.

The tacks may also be used in the event that the rawhide is to be held into place with rawhide thongs. If the drum is to be a double-headed drum, do the same for the other end of the drum.

Begin to stretch the hide tightly, by pulling and either tacking the stretched head in place, or by pulling the rawhide thong as tightly as it will allow. When creating a single headed drum, the thong may be either attached to pegs, holes or tacks near the bottom of the frame, or go under the edge of the frame. Then attach to the holes in the rawhide directly opposite the starting hole, working it's way around the frame so that the back of the frame re-

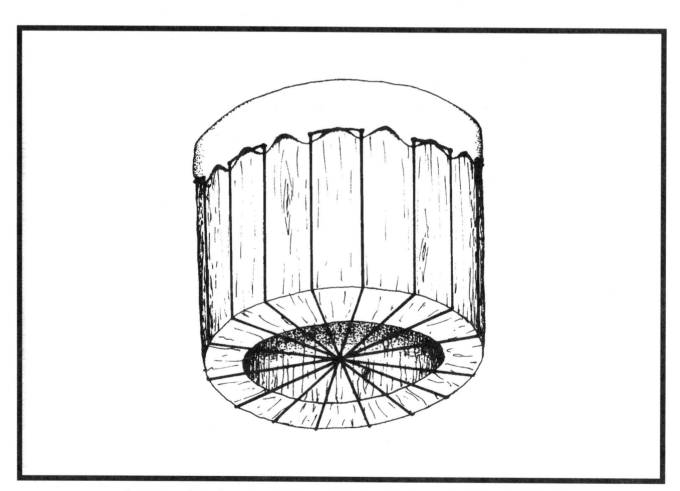

Bottom of Lacing should Resemble the Spokes of a Bicycle Wheel

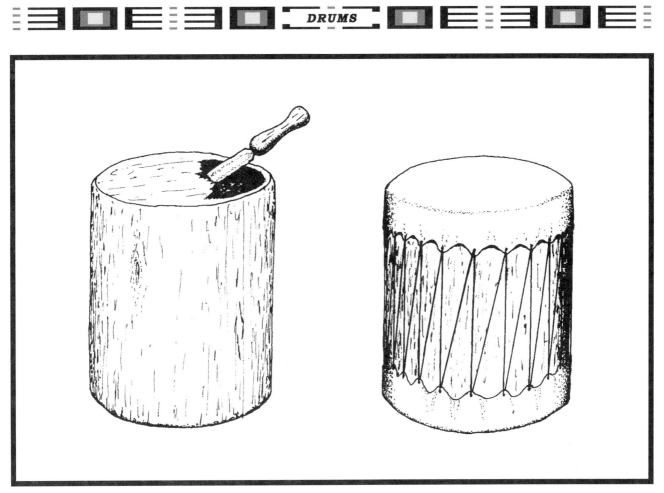

Construction of a Southwest Style Drum

sembles the spokes of a bicycle wheel. If the drum is a double-headed drum, then the rawhide thongs will go from bottom to top. Be sure that the thong is kept equal around the heads as the rawhide is run around the perimeter of the frame. It is much easier to loosely lace the two heads together and tighten the thongs after both heads are placed. Simply continue to pull the thongs more tightly each time the drum is rotated. It would not be uncommon to tighten the rawhide thongs as many as twenty times on a large drum.

As the rawhide dries, the pitch of the drum will rise. It is at this point that mas-ter drum makers are separated from the beginners. Learning exactly how tight a head should be laced to the frame to get a particular pitch, or sound, takes years of practice. The Taos People practice for years and the best drums that they make sell for thousands of dollars. The cost is obviously not in the value of the cottonwood frame nor the rawhide from cow, deer, elk or horse, but rather compensation for the practiced knowledge of a great drum maker.

BOX DRUMS

In the colder northern climates, raw-

Northwestern Cedar Box Drum

hide is not a practical material for a drum head as the drum would need to be constantly kept near a fire or it would rapidly lose it's tone; therefore, drums made entirely of wood are common.

A five-sided "box" is made from whatever wood may be available. Hardwoods, such as oak, walnut, hickory, etc. are the most desirable. The box may be made in nearly any shape or size, some having been observed as long as three feet deep and wide and ten feet in length!

The open end of the box is covered or closed with a single piece of softer wood, such as cedar or spruce, or a harder material such as birch or mahogany. The wood "head" may be beaten with fists or a well padded mallet. If the drum is handheld and small, fingers may be adequate. In some cases, the drum is so large, that the drummers will lay the drum box on the

Clay Pot Water Drum

ground with the "head" vertical to the ground or floor, sit on the box frame and drum with their feet.

WATER DRUMS

Another type of drum is the water drum. This drum is predominantly used in Southwestern cultures and is also used by singers in the Native American Church.

A pot six to twelve inches in diameter is required, with a piece of brain tanned

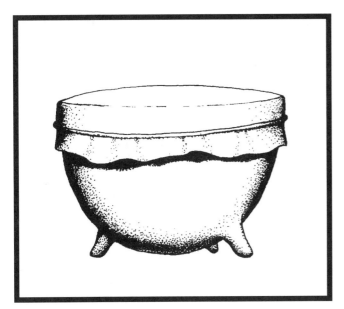

Pueblo Style Water Drum

deer hide, a length of deer hide or elk hide thong and water. The tanned deer hide and thong are kept inside the pot when the drum is not in use.

To use the drum, the pot must be filled with water until it is about one-quarter full. Dip the tanned hide into the water, working the water into the skin until it is thoroughly soaked. Pull the hide over the top of the pot and tightly tie the thong around the neck of the pot. Go around the neck at

least two times with the thong. Before tying the thong off, pull the hide as tightly as possible. Playing the drum will cause the head to dry out a bit, causing the pitch to rise. If the pitch rises higher than desired, simply splash water inside the pot against the head; this causes the head to be rewet and, consequently, this will lower the pitch.

NAC WATER DRUM

The drum used by the Native American Church is made from a cast iron pot with the handle ears filed off but uses the same brain tanned head as the pot drum described above. The head is held on using seven rocks or marbles under the cover as lugs. These 'lugs' are held in place by tying the tie cord around each lug, going under the legs of the pot and catching the cord on the other side. When the tie is complete, the seven lugs are evenly spaced, representing a star or peyote button, de-

Native American Church Water Drum

This Edward Curtis 1927 Photo Shows the Native American Church Water Drum in Use

The Head of the NAC Water Drum is Rewet to Tune the Pitch

pending on the individual point of view.

EASTERN PLAINS WATER DRUM

Indigenous people of the Eastern Plains and Woodlands used trunks of trees instead of pots for their water drums.

A log is cut to the desired length and hollowed out so that the walls are approximately one inch thick. A round "plug" that will fit into, and close, the bottom section of the drum is needed. This plug is then fit into place and sealed with several coats of pine pitch. A band of wet rawhide is then stretched around the bottom section and secured with a stick. It is then twisted several times until the band is very tight. When this rawhide band dries and shrinks, the bottom of the drum will be extremely tight.

As with the pot water drum, the log water drum uses a tanned skin rather than a rawhide head. The drum frame is filled to one-quarter full. The head is held in place either by a cedar hoop forced over the top of the drum or by a leather thong. Again, the head is soaked, pulled very tightly over the frame and tuned by splashing water against the head from the inside.

Drums may be decorated in many different ways. They are often painted with scenes from individual dreams or experiences. Animals are also popular subjects for drum painting. In recent times, drums have become collectible works of art, fetching very high prices.

Eastern Style Water Drum

DRUMSTICKS

Drumsticks may be made in any number of ways. The drumstick has a great deal to do with how the drum sounds. A hard stick will make the drum more sharp in timbre and a soft stick will make the drum sound more open and full. Either type of stick works well, however the softer, full sound is considered by most to be more natural. It also allows the drum to exhibit more bass in frequency response.

Historically, drumsticks were merely a stick with rags wrapped around one end; sometimes, with a piece of skin sewed over the rags and tied in place. Some tribes in the Southwest and Northeast use a stick with the drumming end bent in a full circle.

The portion of the circle furthest from the stick is the part of the stick used to strike the drum head. As more sturdy materials became readily available, sticks radically changed. Drums became more powerful sounding and the number of drummers increased to make the drum even more present.

Fiberglass rods of various lengths can be purchased at most Native craft supply stores; this is the most common material used by pow wow drum groups today. In the past, old fishing rods were cut down to the desired length. For pow wow style sticks, they are usually cut from eighteen to twenty-six inches in length. Hand drum sticks are usually ten to sixteen inches in length. The longer the stick, the more power it has, but it is also more difficult to maintain a consistent rhythm with a longer stick.

The end of the rod is wrapped with a soft material, and covered with leather or electrical tape. Some drummers use neoprene obtained from sporting goods stores

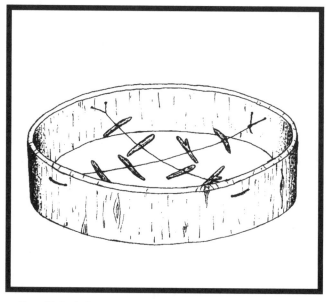

Small Sticks Create Rattles Inside the Drum

to wrap the striking end. They then finish off the neoprene with thin leather, giving the stick a large, flat and soft surface.

When working with fiberglass rods, it is advisable to cover all of the stick with either leather and/or electrical tape, so that splinters of glass are prevented from flying free in the event of stick breakage.

Wooden doweling, 3/8" to 7/8" also works well for drumsticks, particularly sticks for hand drums. Dowels can be purchased at most hardware and grocery stores for a nominal price. The manufacture and finish of these wooden sticks is the same as with the fiberglass stick, although it is not necessary to cover the entire stick with leather or tape.

Sticks used for Northeastern drums and for Dine' song and dance drums are circular at the striking end. The stick is skived thin at one end and then soaked overnight, or until very wet and pliable. The wet wood is then bent around a round object and tied until it dries in position. The wood is then tied, sewn or glued to permanently keep it in place. The overall length of the sticks will vary, depending on the maker. These sticks are not used for pow wow drumming as, while they are not fragile, they certainly will not stand the pressure required for pow wow style drumming. They are used more often as an individual drum stick on a small hand drum. These sticks are not covered with any material, excepting non-functional sticks made for appearances only.

The sticks of the Pueblo people are perhaps the simplest to make. Simply take a straight stick of hard wood, put a 'ball' of soft material on one end and tie a scrap of leather or cloth over the soft ball. Sticks with a "superball," or toy rubber ball, glued

on one end and then leather tied over it are common.

Native American Church (NAC) drums use a stick of hard wood, with no padding whatsoever. Usually twelve to fourteen inches long, some are plain while others are elaborately carved in shallow relief. Only one stick is used.

Drumsticks are often decorated, and it is very beautiful to see several drummers with sticks decorated in a similar manner, with all sticks rising and falling at the same moment. The sticks themselves become dancers with all colors melding together as a moving rainbow. Painted bands around the stick, tightly wrapped thread similar to the finishes on a fine fishing rod or sections of brightly colored electrical tape wound at measured intervals are all common methods of decorating sticks. Fringed handles are also fairly common, although fringes should not be longer than a couple of inches as they will impede the motion of

Detail of waterdrum stick

the stick; this will cause the drum to be off time. Beaded sticks are beautiful, yet rare, as sticks get a lot of abuse and it would be a shame to damage a work of art such as a beaded drum stick. The old beaded sticks seen in museums are more for decoration, presentation and artistic expression rather than daily use.

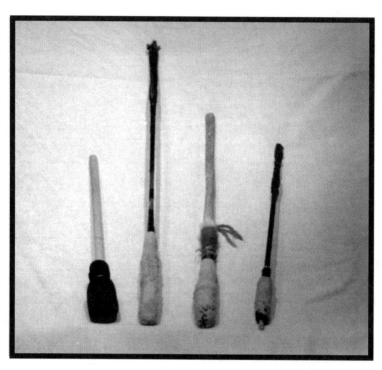

A Collection of Pow Wow Drum Sticks

RATTLES, GOURDS AND SHAKERS

Shaken instruments are common all over the continent and come from every Nation. Gourds, shakers, and rattles are made from every material imaginable, with each nation having it's own traditional form and material of manufacture. Shakers are used to keep musical time at some of the

Fine Examples of Beaded Gourds, a Basket Drum and a Bedoni Style Flute

An Example of a Rattle made from the Shell of a Turtle

Northwestern gatherings, as well as those of the Northeastern Plains. Shakers are not often found at pow wows as the deer toes, jingles, and dance bells keep time for the dancers.

TURTLE SHELL RATTLES

In the Southeastern regions of the country, turtle shells are commonly found as rattles. The shells are about six inches in length, four inches in width and three inches thick. Once the body of the turtle

In this 1832 George Catlin Sketch of Blue Medicine (Sioux) both the
Drum and Rattle are Prominent

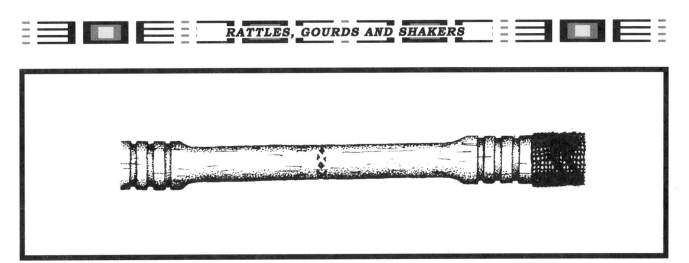

Gourd Sticks may be Decorated with Carving, Paint, Beadwork and other Materials

has been removed, a hollow shell with two openings remains. These shells can be purchased at many Native supply stores. (It should be noted that many species of turtle are protected by federal law. Insure that you are dealing with a reputable person selling legal goods before making any purchase.)

Rawhide or leather may be used to seal the openings, thus preventing the pebbles, corn, teeth, or other hard small "rattles" from falling out. A stick is then pushed through and glued, tied or sewn into place. The handle of the stick may be decorated.

DRIED GOURD RATTLES

Dried gourds also make an excellent shaker. Gourds range in size from one or two inches to the size of a basketball. Gourds that are two to six inches make the most common form of shaker.

A handle or stick cut to the desired length is needed. A dowel will work very well for this. A "button," or flat round object, that is only slightly smaller than the opening in the bottom of the gourd is

needed. This button slides over the handle, preventing the rattle material inside the gourd from falling out. The handle needs to be able to protrude through the gourd at least one-half inch from the top of the gourd so that the handle might be held tight to the gourd body.

Another method is to carve the rattle handle in such a manner as to have the thin end expand into the handle of the body. This eliminates the need for the retaining "button."

Drill a hole in the gourd exactly opposite the opening already in place. This hole should only be large enough to allow the handle to pass through the gourd. Place the button on the handle at the desired location, remembering to have enough length left in the handle to go all the way through the gourd body; be sure to leave enough material to fasten the handle to the gourd body. Place beads, stones, corn, or other hard material inside the gourd, with the gourd on it's side. Push the handle into place. Using glue, leather or yarn, tie a knot or wrap lengths around the portion of the handle protruding from the top of the gourd. This will keep the handle in place. By using the tied material at the top of the gourd/ stick, this allows the gourd to be removed from the stick at any time so that the material inside the gourd might be changed; this also allows the handle of the gourd to be decorated or changed.

COWHORN RATTLES

Cowhorn, cut off at both ends, plugged with either wood or rawhide, makes a great rattle/shaker. Scrape or sand off all of the excess outer horn until the outer wall of the horn is smooth and attractive. A belt sander with fine sandpaper is a good power tool for this task. If more traditional methods are desired, a chunk of sandstone may be used, or even a sharp piece of obsidian, for scraping. The thinner the walls of the horn, the more bright and loud the shaker will be. Once the desired appearance and tone are achieved, cut the tip and bottom rim of the horn off so that both ends are squared off and smooth.

Trace the ends of the horn onto a thin piece of wood. Cut out the shape and whittle or sand the wood plugs into a shape that will fill each end of the horn. Once the ends fit tightly, place rattle materials into the horn and plug both ends with the pieces just made. The end plugs may be

Dance Rattle Made from Cowhorn

either glued into place or small pegs made from toothpicks may be pounded into the wood plug after holes have been drilled or burned into the horn.

A horn shaker will work without a handle, but if a handle is desired either end (or both ends) may be drilled out and a handle attached with one of the many methods described earlier in this chapter.

74

RAWHIDE/BLADDER RATTLES

Rawhide or bladder is another material traditionally used to make a shaker/rattle. Rawhide is very malleable and can be shaped to make an unlimited number of designs. Rawhide from cow, horse, deer, elk or goat are most commonly used. The thinner the rawhide, the more bright the sound of the rattle. Bladder material is extremely thin and very translucent; this makes for a quiet, yet fairly bright, sound. Bladder material may be obtained from most Native American craft suppliers or from the local slaughter house.

The rawhide is cut into either one or more shaped pieces that, when sewn together, create the desired form. A pair of matched round pieces are a good shape with which the beginner might start.

Soak the rawhide pieces in warm (not hot) water until the rawhide is very limp and pliable. Using nylon thread, artificial sinew or rawhide thongs, sew the two sides together; a traditional rattle would be sewn with sinew. Begin at the portion of the rawhide

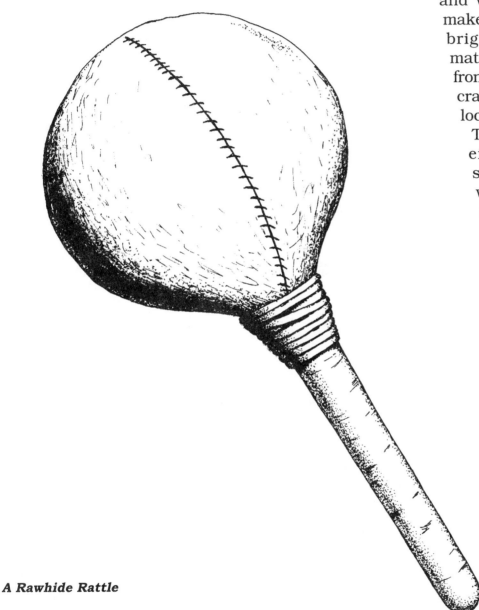

A Rawhide Rattle

body at which the handle shall be attached. In the event that the rawhide is too thick, and it is not possible to push a large needle through the material, a hole punch could be used to pre-punch the holes. Make sure your stitches are not more than 1/4 inch apart, or the next step will not easily be accomplished. When stitching the body together, decoration may be applied over the stitches using a 1/2" wide strip of otter or rabbit fur. Stitch the fur into place with the same thong or thread used to close the body of the rattle. The combination of fur

and alternated stitching is very attractive. The fur may also be attached after the bag has been stitched, shaped, and dried.

Using a funnel, or by just careful pouring, fill the wet rawhide "bag" with fine sand. The sand should be pushed into the bag with a blunt stick to compact the sand and keep the bag taut. This will prevent the rawhide from shrinking out of shape as it dries. The sand also allows for the rattle body to be shaped and formed to the makers imagination. Allow the rawhide body to dry completely.

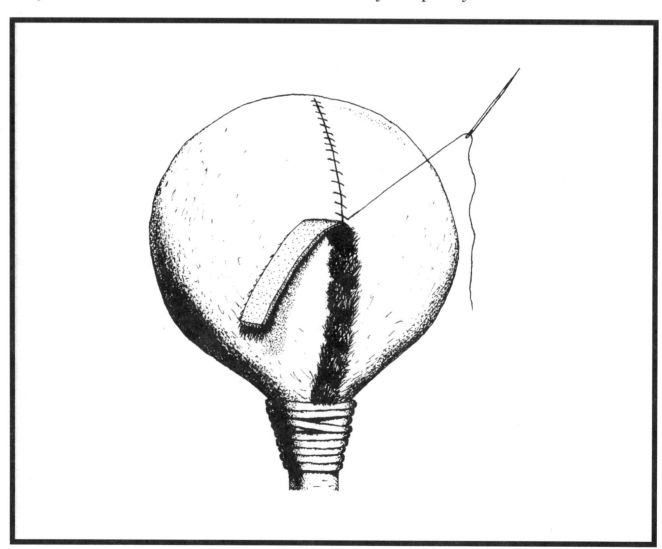

Fur is Often Used to Decorate Rawhide Rattles

A Traditional Rawhide Rattle

Once the body is dry, the sand is removed by shaking and prodding until the compacted sand loosens and may then be poured out. Now the handle can be fitted to the body. The handle only protrudes into the rawhide body a couple of inches, causing the handle of a rawhide rattle/shaker to be shorter than that of a gourd or turtle shell rattle/shaker. Fit the handle into the opening left in the rawhide body, making sure that the fit is tight If it is not tight, the rattle material will fall free.

Popcorn seeds, small rocks, metal or glass beads, BB's or plastic pellets all make good rattle material. The harder and more uneven the rattle material is, the brighter the sound of the rattle/shaker will be. Place the rattle material into the body, shaking the body from time to time, until the desired sound is achieved.

Soak the unsewn end of the bag in water until it is soft and pliable. Put the handle into the opening and secure it to the body by tightly stitching the opening around the handle. Or, to avoid re-soaking the bag, use glue or wet rawhide thongs wrapped around the opening. You may also use leather strips, cut very thin and stretched very tightly around the handle and the body opening.

METAL SHAKERS

Small tin cans and aluminum salt shakers are also often used to make shakers/rattles. They are quite loud and usually very bright in tone. Veteran dancers, or "gourd" dancers, often use this kind of shaker for it's volume.

A tin can, such as an evaporated milk can, that has been drained by punching a hole in one end may be made into a rattle in a similar fashion as a gourd. Once the can is empty, rinse it out thoroughly and allow the can to dry. Then enlarge the hole in the end of the can to accommodate the handle. If a decoration at the top of the rattle is desired, such as horse hair, feathers, yarn or bead work, punch a hole at the opposite end of the handle hole. Be sure that the handle has adequate length to go all of the way through the can body.

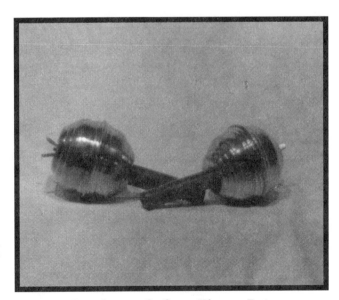

Rattles made from Flower Pots

Secure the can to the handle by means of hot glue, epoxy, pegs pushed through the handle top or simply by using a leather thong around the portion of the handle extended through the top of the can/body.

An examination of the illustrations in this and the following chapter will give the reader some excellent ideas on how to attach handles to gourds and rattles.

A salt shaker is used in much the same manner, only the punctured (pouring) end of the salt shaker attaches to the handle. Again, the handle may go through the top of the salt shaker for decorative purposes and greater stability. With the salt shaker body, the pouring part of the body attaches permanently to the handle by means of epoxy or hot glue. The threads on the body and lid of the shaker allow the body of the rattle to be removed at any time.

OTHER RATTLES

CORN HUSK RATTLES

Rattles may be made from corn husks also. These rattles, while not long lasting, are quick and simple to make and they were, therefore, quite common in more traditional times.

A short stick, a few dried corn husks, and some dried kernels of corn are needed. If husks are difficult to obtain due to the time of year, the local grocery store will have

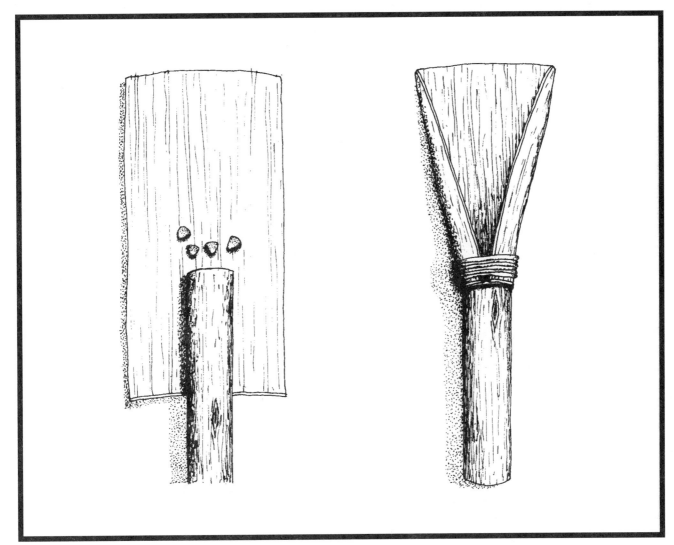

A Corn Husk Rattle

A Completed Drum Stick Rattle

packaged dried husks in their ethnic foods section. Popcorn could be used as a substitute for regular corn kernels.

The husk is folded in half and then a few kernels of corn placed in the center of the inside of the fold. The stick is then inserted into the open bottom of the husk and string, sinew or wetted husk is used to tie the bottom of the husk tightly to the stick. When the bottom is tied off the open sides of the husk naturally close and will stay that way. The rattle is now complete.

DRUMSTICK RATTLES

Particularly in the Northeast, the various Nations had a stick that was rounded into itself as a standard drum stick (see "drumsticks"). At some point in time, a player came upon the idea of filling the open wooden void with pebbles and covering the stick head with rawhide. A rattle/drumstick combination was the result. This instrument/tool makes a great sound when used in conjunction with a large or small

drum as it creates three sounds at once. The drum has it's own deep voice, the harmonic of the stick striking the drum has it's own sound, and the rattle adds another voice to the expression.

OTHER RATTLES

These are just a few of the materials that may be used to make shakers and imagination is the only limiting factor. Shakers have been made from butterfly cocoons, seed pods, hollowed out bits of wood, tin tinkles, rifle shells (particularly .22 caliber), bark, wicker basketing, ceramic material, coconut shells, cowhorn, antlers and nearly anything else that might be a closed vessel. Once, at a hand game in Montana, players were observed using boxes of macaroni and cheese. Imagination,

truly, is the only limiting factor.

DEER TOE RATTLES

Deer toes or dew claws (the nail material found between the back of the knee and hoof of a deer leg), suspended on a stick are another traditional form of rattle/ shaker. The toes, striking each other, make for a dull, rhythmic sound.

Toes (actually the toe nail as the toe bone is removed), are available from nearly any Native American craft supply or at a local meat packing house during the hunting season. If the raw toes are obtained from the meat packing house, they must be thoroughly cleaned of all flesh, hair and blood; if this is not done, the toes will develop a very offensive odor. Be sure to completely remove all bone material, leaving

A Traditional Crow Rattle[2]

Gourd Rattle, Deer Toes & Bone Flute

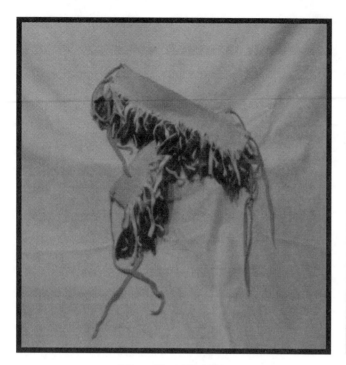

Deer Toe Rattles

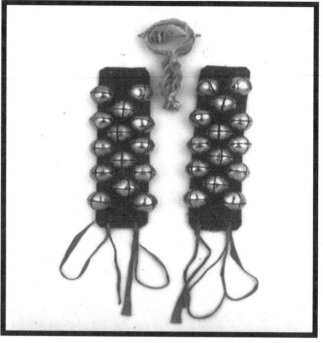

Dance Bells with a Rawhide Rattle

only the husk or nail portion of the toe. Dew claws will slip free of the bone quite easily, making the cleaning much more simple than cleaning the toe. Toe nails are much more desirable in terms of volume and quality of sound and really are worth the extra effort required to clean them.

Once the prepared toes or claws are in hand, the pointed end, or the tip of the toe, must be pierced. This can be accomplished through a variety of methods; burning or drilling being the most common.

Heat a thin strand of metal (such as a cut length of clothes hanger) on a stove, over a candle or fire, or perhaps using an old soldering iron. Apply the hot tip to the toe or claw pushing the tip into the toe fiber. The hot metal will melt it's way through the toe very quickly. At this point, the odor of burning hair is obvious so this effort may best be taken outside where the odor will not permeate furnishings. This method is the most traditional and creates a clean hole.

Drilling, while less troublesome, will work with a 1/16th to 1/8th inch drill bit; however, unless the bit is very sharp, more often than not the toe will split, chip or break, rendering it useless. The odor is present whether drilling or burning the toes.

Cut a stick or a piece of 1/2 inch doweling to the desired length. The deer toes should cover approximately half of the overall stick. The stick may be painted, covered with buckskin or left in it's natural state. The stick should be decorated before attaching the deer toes to it. Fringe on either, or both, ends is very attractive, or trade wool in either blue or red, stitched

over the length of the handle is also very nice.

After decorating the stick/handle, drill 1/8 inch holes no farther apart than 1/2 inch. Drill half the number of holes as there are toes; i.e.; thirty toes equals fifteen holes. Knot the end of a three inch leather thong and run it through a deer toe. Put the free end of the thong through one of the holes in the stick, put the same free end through another deer toe and tie another knot. This attaches two toes to the stick. Repeat this process until all the holes have toes attached to them. Since the holes drilled are 1/2 inch apart, the toes strike each other when the stick is moved.

Decorating the shaker makes for a showy appearance as well as making the shaker/gourd a work of art. Decoration may be as simple as painting the handle or body, or as elaborate as beading the handle. It may be finished by incising and painting the gourd or rawhide and adding plumage to the top of a gourd. Short fringes on the bottom of the shaker handle are attractive; however, if the fringing is too long then the instrument will be difficult to play with any reasonable timing. As with painting, beading or decorating any object of art, be sure the decoration is original in form and not a copy of an artifact found in a museum or collection. Music is an individual expression of emotion and so should be the instruments creating that expression.

DEER TOES AND LEG BELLS

Trappers and traders began carrying bells into the lands of the upper Missouri River in the mid 1800's forever changing

Salt Shaker Rattles

Old Style Dance Bells

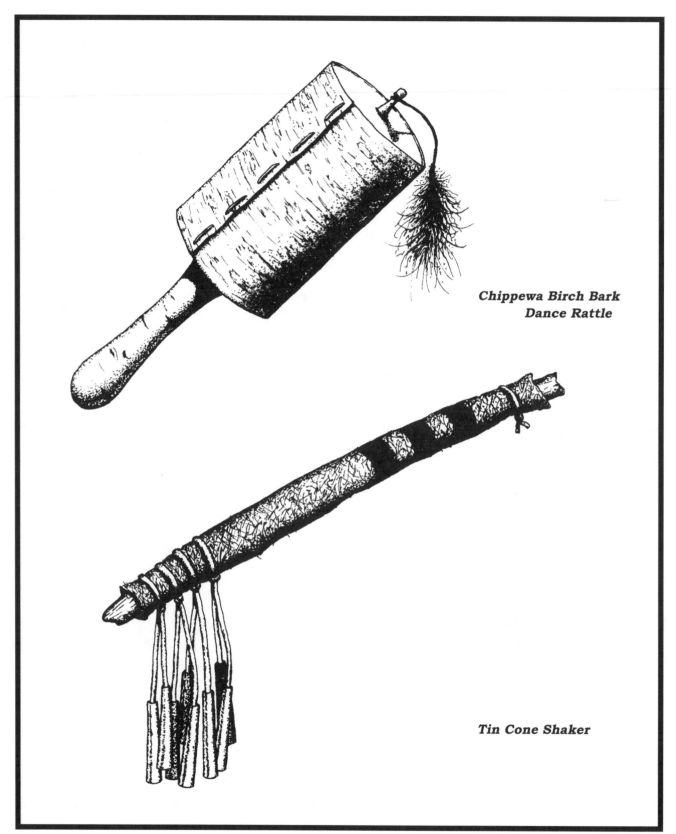

Chippewa Birch Bark
Dance Rattle

Tin Cone Shaker

the sounds heard at social gatherings. However, leg- and ankle-worn rhythm instruments were common long before the advent of non-indigenous adventurers.

Deer toes were the original leg-worn rhythm instruments of the Plains peoples as they were readily available, easy to replace and the sound is very gentle, yet piercing. Bandoliers of deer toes and dew claws are still commonly found at pow wows in contemporary times. Museum studies suggest that the bandoliers were originally used to decorate a horse's neck and evolved into a pow wow accouterment.

The deer toes were pierced by a hot object, such as a stick with a burning ember on it. A bit of leather or rawhide tied through the hole and the toe, or dew claw, was ready for attachment. Modern tools have not greatly improved upon the old method. The dew claws and toes are very thin and brittle and attempting to use a power drill usually results in split toes. A soldering gun, wood burning tool or heated bit of clothes hanger will quickly pierce the cuticle. A short bit (4-6 inches) of buckskin, cord or string knotted and passed through the toe makes it very simple to attach the toe to a base material. To make a pair of leg worn rattles at least twenty toes or dew claws are required. If dew claws are to be used, then a great number are needed to generate any audible sound. Most leg worn rattles made from toes contain approximately fifty toes per leg.

The base material is generally leather, approximately three to four inches in width, and the length depends upon the diameter of the wearer's ankle or calf. Depending on the number of toes to be used, holes are punched no further than one inch apart in any direction. The string or thong is then passed through the punched hole, brought through the next hole in the base, passed through another toe and then knotted. In this manner, it allows two toes to share one thong. It is important that the string, or thong, length be similar on all toes so that the toes strike each other when moving. This is what generates sound and the greater the number of toes, the louder the sound will be.

Once the base is covered with the desired number of toes, a pair of thongs may be attached to each end of the base. These are used to tie the instrument to a leg or ankle.

Deer toes may generally be purchased from various trading posts, Native craft suppliers or even at a meat packing house during the hunting season. If all else fails, goat toes may be substituted for deer toes. Goat toes are commonly used in South American countries as a hand held rhythm device and can be found through most music stores as a percussion instrument.

Tin Cone Leg Shaker[2]

Deer Toe Bandolier

WHISTLES

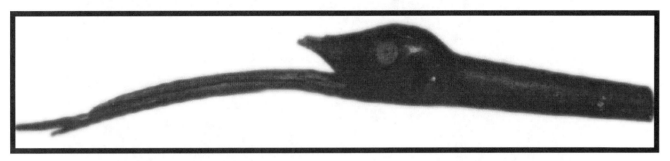

Grass Dance Whistle (circa 1900) - Note that Upper Beak has Broken Off

Many of the early grass dancers used whistles made from wood, similar to a flute, yet usually much smaller in size and length. Most of the early whistles had no finger holes so the whistle could be held in the mouth and simply blown during the dance.

In contemporary times the wooden whistle is rarely seen, although grass dancing is more popular than ever. The grass whistle seems to be predominantly gone with only a few grass dancers still using the whistle. In fact, the only wooden whistles seen in contemporary times have been in parts of Canada.

The wooden whistle is a two chambered length of wood, rarely longer than eight to ten inches in length. The end of the whistle often is elaborately carved in the shape of a bird. Sometimes a fluff of eagle feather is either tied tightly to the end or dangled beneath the end of the whistle.

A piece of wood, typically cedar, is cut to length. The wood is then split in half, and the divided sections hollowed out equally on each length. It is very important that the split be clean, but not necessarily straight, or the two halves will not properly mate when they are completely hollowed out.

The two halves are each hollowed out in each chamber, making the walls of the chamber as thin as possible. The thinner the wall of the chamber, the brighter and louder the whistle will be.

White Snow Goose Whistle of Carved Wood[1]

Crane's-head Whistle[1]

89

George Catlin made this Sketch of Silver Spur (Apache) in 1832
Note Whistle on Necklace

The two halves are then put back to-gether and bound with wet rawhide, sinew or glued so that the two sides are tight and free from escaping air.

It should be noted that the wooden whistle, as used in the older times, was not used to honor a song or a drum and, there-fore, blowing it did not give the player the right to ask that a song be contin-ued beyond it's normal length. Blowing the whistle while dancing was only for the dancer's pleasure, to demonstrate his pride and for the enjoyment of the dance.

While it is true that whistles are also made from eagle wing bone, or sometimes goose

wing bones, the description for making them is not shown here for reasons ex-plained below.

Bone whistles were used in older times as a signal in battle, as a helper in the sundance arena and for the *heyoka* to call for the thunder. Omaha leaders, of which there are only four, are also permitted the use of the whistle. The whistles are often improperly used in contemporary times by nearly anyone who has the ability to make one. The whistle, traditionally, is used only by *heyoka* outside of the sundance arbor and should not be brought into the pow wow arena. According to elders at Pine

Ridge, Rosebud, Rocky Boy and Fort Belknap, using the whistle, by anyone other than the *heyoka* and outside of the sundance arbor, is disrespectful and im-proper.

While many readers may be of good heart, and have only the best of intentions, to duplicate these instruments used only for special pur-poses is not ap-propriate. At best, it is disre-spectful and at worst, it is mock-ing a sacred rite. Depending on the religious per-spective of the reader, it is also often said that trifling with things best left to their sacred na-ture, might re-sult in severe harm to those that would abuse such items. Many of the elders interviewed about this subject, from areas all around the Northern Plains, felt that when the dancers use these whistles in the pow wow arena what the dancer is really crying for is personal attention. These elders say that only sun dancers should be permitted the use of the whistle outside the *wi wacipo* arbor. From another view, native culture is evolving within itself and the people are assimilating the traditions of other Nations into their own lives. Therefore, there will always be disagreement with regards to what was once for sacred use only and what is now considered acceptable privilege. In

the words of Sam Moves Camp (*Woptura Ti Ospaye* - Lakota), "This whistle is not for anyone but the *heyoka*, or the Omaha, to use outside of the sundance arena. To do so is not reverent, and shows that the dancer doesn't care for the culture of others, nor his own culture."

RASPS AND BULLROARERS

Rasps are found in many different cultures and the indigenous people of North America are no different. The rasp is similar to the *guiro* or *morache* of the Hispanic cultures, yet most indigenous rasps are not tubed with notches, but rather flat with notches.

The instrument is not very loud when played solo and therefore a basket, turtle shell, drum, dried hollow pumpkin or gourd was often used to amplify the sound. The end, or bottom, of the rasp is held in place on top of the amplifying device and then scraped in time with the rhythm. At large social gatherings, several rasps would be played at the same time for volume as well as encouraging several people to participate in the occasion.

Hardwood or antler are great materials from which to create the rasp body. Soft woods such as pine, willow, poplar, etc. will split or crack under the pressure of the rasp. Soft woods will also lose the notch edges more quickly.

Rasp designs may vary from simple sticks similar to the size of a ruler, to larger

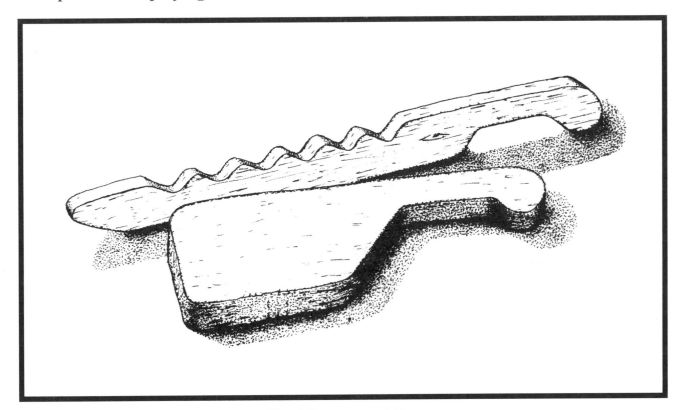

Wood Scraper and Rasp

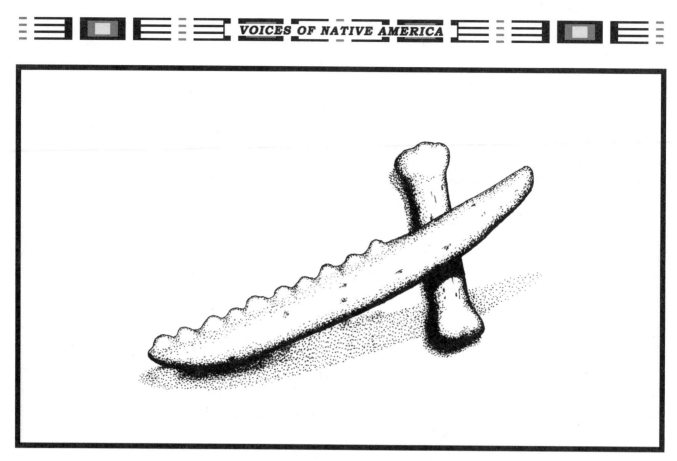

Rasp and Scraper Made from Bone

more elaborate works of art. Many of the old style rasps have a bird head carved into either the rasp body or the scraper stick; however, there is no proper or improper design in creating a rasp.

Once a design has been determined, draw a pattern on a length of wood 1/2 inch to 3/4 inch thick. Rasps are traditionally eighteen to twenty-four inches in length and 1 1/2 to 2 1/2 inches wide. Using a band saw, coping saw or knife, cut the wood into the desired shape. Take special care not to cut the notches too deep into the body or it will be difficult to rub the scraper across them. The notches should be approximately one-half inch deep and less than one-half of an inch apart.

Once the body is cut out, lightly sand

it to remove the rough edges. The notches should be smooth to make the scraper easy to move with constant contact to the face of the rasp. The tone of the rasp is best when the notch edges are slightly beveled to a width of about 3/8 inch.

The scraper may also be made from any number of materials; however, as mentioned above, hard wood is the preferred material. Deer or elk antler tip may also be used. The scraper needs to be long enough to allow the player to hold it without their fingers being too close to the rasp body, yet not so long that it is cumbersome. Eight to ten inches in length is average.

Rasps are not commonly decorated with additional objects, but rather simply engraved, burned or painted. Additional

adornments would only be obstructive to the performance.

BULLROARERS

Bullroarers are found in limited numbers across most of North America but they are prevalent in much larger numbers in the Southwest. The sound of the bullroarer represents thunder in several cultures but it was also used to attract curious antelope during the hunt. It was used in prayers to attract rain and also as a play toy for children.

The bullroarer is a long slender stick, generally shaped like a feather or a miniature surf board. The stick is suspended from a thirty-six to forty-eight inch string, or thong, that sometimes has a handle or ring attached to the opposite end. When the stick is spun in a circular direction, the stick rapidly rotates creating a moaning drone that speaks as if it were the earth crying. The drone provides a soothing contrast to other percussion instruments in an ensemble performance.

To make a bullroarer, a thin piece of soft wood is needed that is twelve to fifteen inches long, 1 1/2 to 2 1/2 inches wide and approximately one-quarter inch thick.

The stick is cut or carved into the desired shape and then one side is beveled or rounded off. The opposite side should be kept as flat as possible.

The wide end of the bullroarer will need a hole drilled into it in order to accept the thong or string; the thong should be approximately one-quarter inch in diameter.

Apache Bullroarer with Side View Shown

Braid together three strands of artificial sinew, that have been cut to a forty-eight inch length, and tie one end to the bullroarer. The cord must be strong, but thin, as a string that is too thick will not allow the bullroarer to rotate and a string that is too thin will break under the pressure of the swinging instrument.

The opposite end of the string may be attached to a handle, a ring or simply wrapped around the finger. The bullroarer is then twirled in a circle in the air. After a few moments, the string will be wound very tight and the bullroarer will need to be stopped and twirled in the opposite direction. If a constant drone is desired, two players are needed. One will begin shortly after the other so that as one player stops to reverse direction, the other is still rotating his bullroarer.

As mentioned before, little may be done to decorate the bullroarer beyond burning, incising or painting. Red or yellow earth paints available from most art supply stores may be rubbed into the wood giving an aged appearance as well as a traditional base upon which a favorite design may be painted.

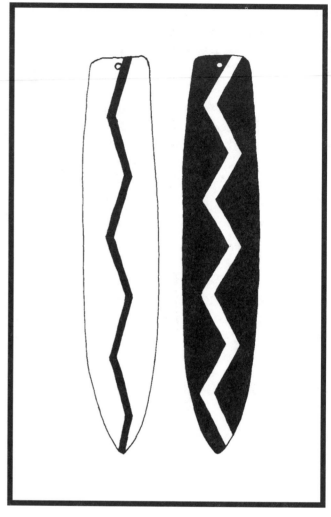

Bullroarer Patterns

SNAPSTICKS AND TAOS SLIT DRUM

Several nations used a stick that had been split with a small section removed. When the stick is slapped against the hand or thigh, it makes a "clacking" noise that is great for keeping rhythm. This instrument is particularly prevalent in the western coastal areas.

A straight, round stick approximately twelve to fourteen inches in length and 3/4ths to one inch in diameter is required. Simply split the stick eight to ten inches down the middle and remove sufficient wood to leave a 1/8 inch gap between the two sides. Wrap leather, artificial sinew or rawhide around the remaining unsplit portion of the stick to prevent further splitting and this completes the handle of this noise-maker.

The stick may be painted or burned for decorating purposes, but care must be taken to assure that both sides of the split portion of the stick remain strong so that they do not break off while the stick is being played.

The snapstick is played by simply slapping the stick against the palm or thigh with one or two being played by each player. Several snapsticks being played at the same time by a large number of players makes a wonderful sound, especially when played in double time to a drumbeat.

TAOS SLIT DRUMS

The Taos and Tewa people of New Mexico have an interesting kind of slit drum

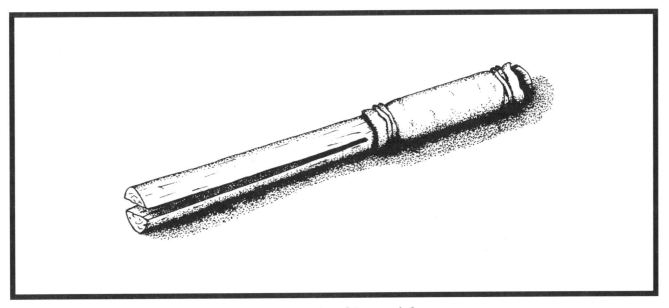

An Example of Snapsticks

that offers two distinct tones to the player. These small, handheld drums are carved from cottonwood which is abundant in that area. Any soft wood will do, although the softer the wood the easier to carve, and the more dull the tone shall be

A tree branch approximately twelve to fifteen inches in length and five inches in diameter is needed. One inch of material is taken off of each side of the branch, leaving a nearly rectangular piece of wood. This is flat on two sides with the other two sides slightly rounded.

Using a knife or bandsaw, cut a handle in one end of the wood. This handle should be no longer than four inches in length. Any longer and the tone of the drum will be negatively affected. Roughly sand the handle area.

Cut one of the flat sides straight off at a depth of 1/2 inch. Save the slab as it will form the head of the drum at a later point in time. The remaining larger portion of wood will become the drum body.

Mark a rectangle around the inside perimeter of the wood, approximately 1/4 inch thick. Use a carving tool to clean all wood from the inside of the drum body until all areas of the body are of equal thickness. In order for the drum to sound the best that it can, the wood must be equal all around the body except for the handle area. The overall appearance should resemble a wooden box with a handle.

The thinner slab must be marked with two "tongues" or feathers of unequal size. These tongues become the drum heads and create the overall pitch of the drum. A coping saw, band saw or small hand saw is used to cut the pattern out of the slab.

The slab is then fitted to the top of the box or body. Make sure that all parts of the slab fit tightly to the body and that there are no gaps. Any gaps will have to be filled in with glue but keep in mind that any large amounts of glue will deaden the sound of the drum as it does not resonate very well.

The Apache violin or fiddle is an instrument that most likely came about as an adaptation of instruments brought over to this continent by the Spaniards. Lack of evidence of the fiddles' existence prior to European contact would seem to support this theory. The fact that the instrument is exclusively social and non-ritual would further support this belief.

The violin is approximately twelve to eighteen inches in length, and may be manufactured from the stalk of the agave or from a dead hardwood tree. There is one incident of a cottonwood fiddle in a museum collection that the author is aware of, however, softwood fiddles appear to be a rarity.

The agave, or tree limb, is split down the middle and the two halves are carved out to create a thin wall. Diamond shapes or round holes are either cut or burned into one half of the two pieces. These holes serve as sound holes. These allow the wood to freely vibrate and release the sound, much like a guitar or standard violin. The body of the violin is then painted or burned with etched or drawn designs. The two halves are then rejoined using rawhide or sinew to fasten them together. Museum pieces indicate either pitch or hide glue was used to further attach the two halves. If the fiddle body is made from the agave, each end of the hollow tube must be plugged and sealed with either pitch or hide glue. Following the joining of the two halves, a hole must

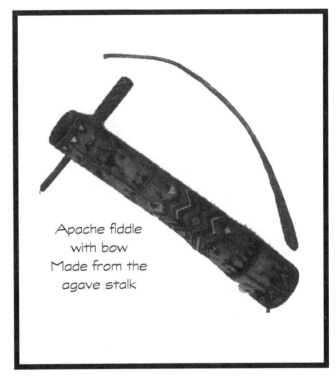

Apache fiddle
with bow
Made from the
agave stalk

be drilled or burned through the entire body which allows a tuning peg to be put in place. Two holes, one at each end of the body, are required for a double strung fiddle.

A tuning peg (or two pegs if the violin is to be double-strung) is then inserted into holes at the top of the body (a peg is also inserted at the bottom of the body if the fiddle is to have two strings). The thinner, or narrower, portion of the instrument is considered to be the top of the body. A small peg is then glued at the end opposite the tuning peg. This small peg becomes the fixed attachment point for the string, with the other end of the string being

Apache Fiddle Player

APACHE FIDDLE

wrapped around the tunable peg.

Strings are generally made from horse-hair or gut, although artifacts having wire strings have been observed. The wire strung fiddles did not play sufficiently to suggest that many fiddles were strung with metal.

The bow is made from sumac or tama-rack. It is generally approximately the same length as the fiddle from curved end to curved end. The bowstring is also of horse-hair.

The tuning of the instrument seems not to be of any great significance although is could easily be assumed that a double strung fiddle would have the two strings a minor third, perfect fourth or perfect fifth apart in pitch. As the instrument is not fretted, rather fingered like a European in-strument, it is primarily a drone instrument not given to melody line. Therefore, the singer would conform his voice to match that of the fiddle in terms of key. Given the tensile strength of horsehair, it would stand to follow that the instrument could not have a pitch much above middle "C".

With no working artifacts from which to attempt to play, and experiments by the author somewhat lacking in perfect results, there is no way to completely understand exactly what the instrument should sound like from a traditional perspective.

Discussion with several members of the Apache Nation gives indication that this instrument enjoyed a fairly brief life in the history of the People. No one interviewed was aware of a fiddle maker or player that is still alive today. Nevertheless, it is an instrument that apparently was popular for a while, even if just a fad of the era, and it is certainly worth mentioning. It's exist-ence seems to fascinate those writing about

Apache fiddle
made from hardwood
Burned and painted decoration

the Apache although most writers decry the fact that the instrument was 'contemporary' in relationship to traditional instruments of 150 years ago.

ADDENDA

Author's Note: Francis Densmore, noted anthropologist and student of Native American cultures, wrote the following three monographs in the early 1900s. These have been chosen as they present some very interesting observations about the Voices of Native America.

CERTAIN PECULIARITIES OF INDIAN MUSIC

STATEMENT of A. H. Fox Strangways concerning the music of Hindostan is applicable to the music of the American Indians. Mr. Strangways says: "One caution with regard to these tunes. It would be a mistake to play them on a keyed instrument; they should be played on a violin, or sung, or whistled, or merely thought. Not only because there is then a hope of their being rendered in natural intonation and of getting the sharp edges of the tones rounded by some sort of portamento, but also because the temperament of a keyed instrument ... has a unique power of making an unharmonized melody sound invincibly commonplace. *'All who are familiar with Native music will admit that it loses its native character when played on a piano. A Native may sing a tone of the same pitch as the piano but his manner of producing the tone and of passing from one tone to another is such that it cannot be imitated on any keyed instrument.'* The only way to preserve an Indian song so it can be generally understood is to transcribe it in the musical notation with which we are familiar, but the best way to learn an Indian song from such a transcription is to hum it, tapping the time on a table or on a heavy book. This will be found more satisfactory than playing it on a piano, even for the purpose of memorizing it. A portion of traditional songs can be harmonized but a very large number belong to the class known as "non-harmonic music" which cannot be harmonized in a satisfactory manner."

Traditional singing differs from our own in that it is not accompanied by an instrument giving gradations of pitch. The singing of the Native is accompanied only by percussion instruments. An accompaniment of three or four drums or rattles is occasionally used but there is no definite pitch among them.

The usual comment on Indian songs is that they begin high, end low, and have more rhythm than melody. Generally speaking, this is correct. Thus in a classification of 1,553 songs, containing 44,061 intervals, it was found that sixty per cent were ascending and forty per cent descending progressions; and, that in sixty-eight per cent the last note was the lowest note occurring in the melody. In a song with steady downward trend the last note is not always the keynote. Sometimes a song with a compass of twelve tones begins on the ninth and ends on the fifth (keynote G, first note A, last note D, in lower octave) while others begin on the twelfth and end on the keynote (keynote G, first note D in upper octave, last note G). It is interesting to note the contrasts between the Native customs and our own. For example, the Indians find their greatest pleasure in chorus singing while we emphasize the singing of solos. When an Indian sings alone at a public gathering it is not because he is a good singer, but because he is singing a song that belongs to him, having been "received from a spirit in a dream," or having some other personal connection. A woman may do the same, occasionally singing the war song of a deceased relative or a song composed in his honor. A doctor may sing alone when treating the sick but he often desires the family or friends of the sick person to join him, not because the sound will be more pleasing but in order that their *orenda* (spirit power/talisman) may supplement his own.

Indians usually sing in a large lodge or in the open air, and the voice of a "good singer" must have a carrying quality not necessary among people who sing in a comparatively small room. The singers at a dance are usually seated around a large drum, beating right lustily upon it as they sing. The leader sings the first phrase of a song softly in order that the others may identify the melody, then the others join him, usually repeating the first phrase, which has served as an introduction. In some tribes the women sing with the men, sitting in a circle a few feet behind the circle of men at the drum. Their heads are covered by their shawls and they often cover their mouths as they sing the melody an octave higher than the men, in a high, nasal tone. They are a strange circle of motionless, shrouded figures, and stranger still is the high, thin tone they produce.

Music among the Indians is essentially a man's occupation. He sings the rituals and ceremonial songs, and treats the sick. In this we find additional evidence of a belief in the power of music. Women are not expected to have the same power as men in accomplishing wonderful things such as bringing rain, calling the buffalo, healing the sick, or talking with the spirits of the dead, although medicine women are not unknown among Natives and are highly respected.

We scarcely realize the extent to which our vocal music is based upon an imitation of a tuned instrument. Comparison with a standardized pitch is unknown among the Indians and they find pleasure in sounds which are not pleasing to our ears. Nevertheless, they have standards of musical excellence not unlike our own. For example, it is required that a good singer have a large repertory and be able to sing a song correctly after hearing it two or three times; he must also have a "convincing quality" in his work, showing a mental grasp of the song. Such a man is leader of the singers. Readiness in learning a song is especially useful when an Indian visits another tribe and wishes to carry home some songs. In my experience, the singers regarded as proficient by their own people have what we call a good intonation, using

the intervals of the diatonic scale with an accuracy that would be considered acceptable in a member of our own race. This accuracy applies especially to the simpler upper partials of a fundamental. The manner of tone production used by the Indians is peculiar to their race. The Indian sings with his teeth slightly separated and motionless, and there is very little change in the position of his lips, the tone seeming to be forced outward by an action of the muscles of his throat. An Indian said, "Something seems to go up and down in my throat when I sing." This forcing of the tone gives it remarkable carrying power. A vibrato is often cultivated and admired. In some tribes there are special qualities of tone for certain classes of songs, the love songs being sung in a peculiar nasal tone, while the lullabies are marked by an upward gliding of the voice before a rest. The Ute gaming songs are marked by an unaccented grace note before the melody tone, the voice sliding upward to the principal tone; and in the Ute songs of the Bear dance there is a sliding downward of the voice. A *glissando* is used in many songs. It is the custom to follow certain songs with vocables or other sounds, the "medicine songs" often being followed by *"Wah———— Hee, hee, hee!"* and the war songs of the Plains by a shrill *"Ki! yi, yi."* The Makah songs concerning the whale are always followed by a long howl, this being given after each song by the men in canoes when towing a dead whale to the shore. The accuracy with which a song is repeated by the Indians was proved by having a song recorded at intervals of considerable time, and also by the recording of the same song by different men. For example, an old man recorded a song in the summer and again in the following winter. A comparison of the two records showed the melody, pitch and tempo to be identical. A similar accuracy was found in songs recorded by a woman after a lapse of three years, the two sets of records being exactly alike. A song is frequently sung eight or even ten times on a phonograph cylinder and the renditions are uniform in every respect. The only exception occurs in songs having several "verses" in which the lengths of the tones vary somewhat with the words. In certain tribes there is a rigid requirement of accuracy in ceremonial songs. If a mistake is made the ceremony must be begun over again and the unfortunate singer must pay a heavy fine. If a man should pretend to know a song and sing it badly he would be severely ridiculed by his people.

The number of songs in the repertory of an Indian is remarkable. I have heard of an Indian who can sing all night for three or four nights, singing each song only four times and not repeating a single song. It is said that many men know three hundred or four hundred songs. I have never tested an Indian to this extent but have recorded more than 200 songs from one singer without any sign of reaching the end of his memory. This is the more astonishing as the Indians have no system of musical notation. The only approach to this is a system of picture-writing in which the Chippewa record the words of the songs of their Grand Medicine Society, a secret organization. There are certain symbols which represent words occurring in the songs, and by the grouping of these symbols the initiated Indian knows what song is intended. He recalls the melody by looking at these little pictures. The songs are in groups of ten, and a member of the society has little strips of birch bark on which are the pictures of the songs, always sung in the same order. **(Author's Note:** Pictographs relating to songs would only be comprehended by members of the same nation, speaking the same dialect, and understanding the close symbology of the drawings. It is similar to a code.)

Very old songs are highly regarded by the Indians and are handed down from one generation to another. Even at the present time the age of a song is reckoned by generations of men, a singer saying that the song belonged to his grandfather or his great-grandfather. It is said that all the old songs were "received in dreams" while modern songs are "composed." Only in a very few tribes are songs being received in the old way at the present time.

The rhythm of Indian songs is characterized by accents which are not evenly spaced, as in songs of the white race, but occur in what often appears to be an irregular manner. When a song is transcribed, a bar is placed before each accented tone and the space between the bars is considered a measure, whether it contains two or five counts and regardless of the number of counts in the measures preceding and following. The Indian sings the rhythm of a song as it was taught to him, but the present writer uses bars and measures because they make the transcription more intelligible. A large majority of Indian songs contain these changes of measure-lengths. At first these changes of time seem erratic, but when the song is regarded as a whole, and especially when it becomes familiar, the changes of measure-lengths are merged in a rhythmic unity which is interesting and satisfactory.

Many Indian songs are thematic in character, one or two themes being worked over in somewhat the same manner that a composer of our own race works over a theme and develops it. In other songs a unit of rhythm is repeated without change throughout the melody. A simple pattern is seen in a song containing four periods of equal or nearly equal length, the rhythm of the first, second and last being the same, while the third period is slightly different. In many Indian songs there is a slight change or "catch" in the rhythm soon after the middle of the song. There are, however, many songs whose rhythm cannot be divided into phrases or periods, the entire song being a rhythmic whole. In a small proportion of songs there is a change of tempo, occurring at the same place in all renditions. Some songs are sung with a slight *rubato* but the Indian usually maintains a metric unit with remarkable regularity, whatever may be the accents in the song. In addition to the foregoing general characteristics of Indian songs there are tribal characteristics, one tribe differing from another in the structure of its songs. The Pawnee songs are lacking in melodic variety, while the Papago songs are tuneful. The Menominee songs are more pleasing and varied than the Chippewa, and the Makah songs are characterized by a small compass, many having a range of only four tones. The songs of the Yuma, Papago, Yaqui and Makah contain more songs without apparent keynote than the songs of other tribes studied by the present writer, these songs being regarded as pure melody without tonality. Indians recognize differences in musical ability among the tribes, saying that such-and-such a tribe "sings a great deal and has good songs."

Tribes differ in the use of rests. Thus

in three hundred and forty Chippewa songs there is scarcely a rest and one wonders how and where the singer takes breath in the long melodies; while in the Cocopa and certain other tribes the rests are frequent and are clearly given in all renditions of the songs. The songs of the Seminole contained a "period formation" found also among the Choctaw in Mississippi and the Tule Indians of Panama. This occurred in a few of the oldest songs, and was also found in Yuma and Pueblo songs. A large majority of male voices among the Indians are baritone in range, while the voices of the women usually are alto or contralto in compass, sometimes extending down to E, third space in the bass clef. The song with largest compass recorded by the writer is a Sioux song with a range of seventeen tones. The songs connected with the playing of games are usually smaller in compass than other classes of songs and contain short phrases, separated by short rests.

It is interesting to note a statement by Major John Wesley Powell, Director of the Bureau of American Ethnology at the time of its organization. Dr. Powell regarded rhythm as the first element of music and assigned it to the "hunter stage" of man's development, stating that "passing from the hunter stage to the shepherd stage we find that a new element is added to music; then melody appears fully fledged . . . So music was endowed first with rhythm and then with melody." It appears to the writer that the elaboration of rhythm is an earlier phase of music as a cultivated art among primitive people.

TECHNIQUE IN THE MUSIC OF THE AMERICAN INDIAN

Music should be recognized as a phase of the culture of the American Indian. When this is done we are ready to look for standards of excellence as in other phases of culture. These are not found as easily in music as in such arts as pottery and basketry. The Indians cannot describe their music in detail and little beyond a general knowledge is gained by listening to the singing at ceremonies, games, and dances. Information must be gained by patient investigation and the Indian often tells a great deal when he is unconscious that he is giving important facts.

The present consideration will be limited to technique in the singing of the Indians except when the tempo of the song is different from that of the accompanying instrument. An interesting study could be made of the Indian technique in drumming and the use of other percussion instruments, as well as the more primitive forms of accompaniment, such as clapping the hands. These, as well as whistles and other wind instruments, are familiar to students of Indian music. The following are phases of technique that are common to many tribes:

Tone production. — The Indian produces his singing tone by a peculiar action of the muscles of his mouth and throat. The writer once sang a Chippewa song for *Main'gans* who had recorded it and asked him if it was correct. He replied, "The tune is right but you haven't an Indian throat." That is the fundamental element in the old Indian singing and cannot be imitated successfully by a white person, neither is it heard in the singing of young, educated Indians. By the use of this peculiar technique an Indian could separate the tones of his song without the use of words or syllables. He could produce note values as short as 32nd notes with distinctness. Among the old Chippewa a peculiar, artificial tone was used in love songs and in no other songs except those of the scalp dance. It is a nasal, whining tone, with a gliding from one pitch to another, and the old love songs can be recognized by this mannerism. It has been compared to the sound produced by an animal and also to an imitation of the sound of a wind instrument. The writer recorded numerous love songs prior to 1911 that were sung with this technique, by both men and women.

A different tone production is used by men who sing around the drum at dances. Theirs is a piercing quality of tone that can be heard a long distance. A similar quality of tone is used by men who make the announcements each evening in a large camp. Such a man was once brought in to make a recording with the statement that he was more than a hundred years old. The writer expected to hear a weak voice, but his voice was astounding in its volume and force. Some men can sing in falsetto, and there are men who have their own manner of tone production that is admired. Thus songs were obtained in 1911 from a young Chippewa who came down from Canada to

Red Lake, in Minnesota, to attend a celebration. He sang with a peculiar throaty vibrato and said that he discovered his ability to do this when a child and had cultivated it ever since. It is heard in the records of his songs. Use of words — This custom differs in various regions. For example, the Chippewa use few words in their songs-only enough to indicate the idea. One of their old songs is in honor of a warrior named Cimau'ganic and the only words were translated "Cimau'ganic killed in war." In such a song the name of a popular hero may replace that of an old warrior, the words of praise remaining the same. Such words generally occur in the middle of the melody, the remainder of the tones being sung with the native tone production requiring no words. In contrast, the songs of Santo Domingo Pueblo contain words through the length of the melody, often describing in detail a custom, such as that of bringing in a harvest of corn from the field.

Accuracy in repeating a melody. — In certain ceremonial songs it is required that a song be repeated if there is the slightest mistake in its rendition. The writer has recorded many repetitions of dance songs in which there was not the slightest difference. This custom however, is not universal. In a series of renditions of a song by a good singer there are often short, passing tones and by-tones. These are permissible to a good singer, as in our own race. In one tribe many differences were noticed in the renditions and the singer was asked to record the song only once. He did so, and a simple melody was heard instead of the rather elaborate versions that he had been recording. In reply to the writer's question, he said that he intended to sing it a

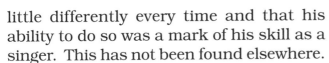

little differently every time and that his ability to do so was a mark of his skill as a singer. This has not been found elsewhere.

Improvisation. — This custom has been recorded in only one tribe, but was connected with folk stories which have not been a subject of special study. It was found among the Northern Ute and several examples were recorded. In these instances the entire folk tale was sung instead of spoken. The melodies contained no rhythmic units nor repetitions of phrases yet the singing of each story had an individuality that was, in some way, characteristic of the actors in the tale. Thus a story about the prairie dogs was expressed in an agile melody and the song about the bear who stole the wolf's wife was sung to a slow, simple melody. The story about the wolf's little children who won a race was sung to a melody with a compass of 11 tones, moving freely within that compass. Three of these songs were recorded by an aged woman who said that she learned them from her mother, up in the canyon. When she was a little girl her mother sang them to her and told her of the time when "the wolves were people." An additional song of this sort was recorded by another woman who was known as Fanny Provo, but no others were found.

Difference in tempo of voice and drum. — In many recorded songs the tempo (metric unit) of the voice is not the same as that of the drum. A singer may sing in one tempo and beat the drum in a different tempo, or he may sing in one tempo while the drum is beaten in a different tempo, by another Indian. In a comparative analysis of 60 old and 62 comparatively modern Sioux songs, the tempo of voice and drum was different in 31 songs of the former

group and in only 15 songs of the latter group. A similar comparison was not made in any other tribe.

Change of pitch level during renditions of a song. — This peculiarity was found to the largest extent in the songs of Santo Domingo Pueblo, N. Mex., though it occurred also in songs of the Yuma in southern Arizona, the Makah in Neah Bay, Wash., and the Winnebago in Wisconsin. This peculiarity has been widely noted in primitive music and mentioned by writers on that subject. After noting the rise in pitch level in many Santo Domingo songs, the singer was asked whether it was intentional. He replied without hesitation, "Yes, that is the way my grandfather taught me to do when he taught me the songs." He added that the rise in pitch-level was used in the old war songs. In some songs the pitch-level was gradually lowered, the change in both instances being about a semitone, after which the new pitch-level was sustained to the end of the performance. Certain mannerisms are connected with various classes of songs. Thus the dancing songs of the Sioux Sun Dance were sung with a "jiggling" tone. This was heard also in recordings of similar songs by the Northern Ute. The Choctaw of Mississippi use different "shouts" with each class of dance songs. This may be a form of the "hollering" that is a custom of Negro singing and was designated by that name among the Seminole of Florida. Similar "shouts" have not been heard in songs of northern tribes. The syllables *"ho ho ho ho"* are heard in the Chippewa songs of the Midewi'win, occurring during the songs and between renditions. Similar sounds are made by medicine men when treating the sick. War songs in many tribes may be interrupted by sharp cries or explosive sentences, and similar cries may follow the songs. In some widely separated tribes the *labial m*, with the lips closed, is heard during portions of the song. It is apart from the purpose of this brief paper to document the foregoing statements which are described in various books by the present writer, but their occurrence shows a degree of technique among Indians and limited standards of excellence in their musical performances.

The intention of the writer's work has been to discover what music means to the Indian and to describe it from his standpoint. In that work it is necessary to use musical terms that are familiar to musicians of our own race, though they are not accurate. Music is a source of pleasure to Indians, and skill according to their standards is appreciated and honored, but music to them, in its highest sense, is connected with power and with communication with the mysterious forces that control all human life. In that, even more than in the sound of the singing, lies the real difference between the music of the American Indian and that of our own race.

BELIEF OF THE INDIAN IN A CONNECTION BETWEEN SONG AND THE SUPERNATURAL

An important phase of Indian music is known as the dream song, which is common to many tribes. These songs are not composed but are said to come to the mind of the Indian when he has placed himself in a receptive attitude. To this extent the source of the song is not unlike the inspiration sometimes experienced by composers of our own race, but the use of the song is entirely different. Our composer regards the song as a possible source of applause or wealth while the Indian connects it with mysterious power. An old Indian said to the writer, "If a man is to do something beyond human power he must have more than human strength." Song is a means through which that strength is believed to come to him. In this, as in all close study of Indians, the student is hampered by lack of an adequate vocabulary and a knowledge of the idioms of the Indian language. A careful interpreter is necessary, with many patient conferences between the interpreter and the Indian as well as with the student, but the result is worth the effort. For example, if the Indian uses a word meaning "spirit" and it is interpreted as *spirit* the significance is changed and there enters the concept of a material form, so the presence of a spirit may be assumed when it is not in the mind of the Indian. On one occasion the writer was questioning LoneMan, a trusted Sioux informant and singer, concerning information received from a pipe. He was asked whether a spirit entered into the pipe and gave the information. He replied this was not the case, saying that under certain conditions a pipe might "become sacred" and speak to the Indian. Among the Sioux Indians the term

"Wakan" is used in referring to any mystery. The term "Great Spirit" is commonly used as the English equivalent of the Sioux word "WakanTanka," which consists of two adjectives, wa'kan, "mysterious" and tan'ka, "great." Throughout the writer's work the term "WakanTanka" is used. In old times this word was not used in ordinary conversation, as it was held too sacred to be spoken except with reverence and at a proper time. That which remains unspoken must be considered in any study of Indian thought, together with the fact that a "sacred language" is sometimes used by which ideas can be conveyed between initiates without being understood by others. To a white man the term "dream" is connected with unconsciousness, but the Indian term implies an acute awareness of something mysterious. Dreams and their songs may come to an Indian in natural sleep if his mind is conditioned to such an experience, but the first important dream comes to a young man in a fasting vigil. He is alone some silent place, and his mind is passive, as he hopes for an impression to come to him from a mysterious source. The silence becomes vibrant, it becomes rhythmic, and a melody comes to his mind. This is his "dream song," his most individual possession. An aged man once recorded his dream song for the writer, then bowed his head and said tremulously that he thought he would not live long as he had parted with his most precious possession.

The white musician composes songs addressed to his deity. The Indian waited and listened for the mysterious power pervading all nature to speak to him in song. The Indian realized that he was part of nature not akin to it. By means of his dream song and by performing certain acts a man might put himself again in contact with the mysterious powers seen in his dream. Others might know the song from hearing him sing it, but no results would follow if they had the temerity to sing it. Yet a man might share his song, its power and its benefits, if he so desired and if someone were willing to pay the price. A man once offered to record his song to bring rain, saying the writer could bring rain at any time by singing it and that he would still have power to do so. His price was $50, and it is needless to say that his offer was declined. The dream songs of the warriors of former days are sometimes sung in the war dances, the name of the warrior being honored in this manner, and the dream songs of forgotten warriors may remain in use, the name of the warrior being lost and only the song remaining. The bird or animal that appeared to the Indian in his dream was an embodiment, to some extent, of the power that he desired and, by his individual temperament, was best fitted to use. A dream of a bear was especially favored by those who treated the sick, as the bear has such good claws for digging herbs which it eats. With the song, a bear may reveal certain herbs to be used by the medicine man. The warrior may dream of a roving wolf, and the hunter may dream of a buffalo. The creature seen in the dream is often mentioned in the song and may be made known in the man's name. Brave Buffalo, a Sioux who recorded several songs for me, had his first dream when 10 years old and in that dream he saw a buffalo. His Sioux name was Tatan'ka-ohi'tika, meaning "brave buffalo bull," but he was commonly known as Brave Buffalo. Later he dreamed of elk and wolves, and he recorded the songs received

111

in these dreams. Dreams concerning forms of nature may be regarded as more primitive than dreams concerning birds or animals, and songs are received from such powers. Such was the dream of a young man who lived to be an old warrior of the Pawnee. His name was Eagle. As a young man he was afraid of the storm and wept when he heard the thunder, but in a dream the thunder spoke to him slowly and said, "Do not be afraid, your father is coming." He heard the thunder sing, learned the song, and sang it when he went to war. The words are freely translated:

> *Beloved it is good,*
> *He, the thunder, is saying quietly,*
> *it is good.*

The term "thunderbird" is more familiar than the term that carries no implication of a material form. Two of the writer's Sioux singers had dreams in which the thunderbirds assumed the form of men riding on horses. Two Chippewa dream songs were concerning the wind. They were recorded by Ki'miwun, "Rainy," at the remote village of Waba'c'ing, on Red Lake in Minnesota. They appear to be the dream songs of forgotten men, as no origin was ascribed to them. The first was used in treating the sick and the words are evidently concerning the man's dream. They are translated:

> *As the wind is carrying me around*
> *the sky.*

The use of the second song was not known, but it had come down from a former time and was still sung. The words are:

One wind, I am master of it.

A member of the Makah tribe, in northwest Washington, related a dream in which the Southwest Wind appeared to him in the form of a man and sang a song, which he learned. This man was a prominent member of the tribe whose name was Young Doctor. He said the words of this song are not Indian words — they are in no known language, and he called it the "wind language." Passing from songs of the thunder and the wind, we turn to a song of the Yaqui concerning a simpler manifestation of nature. The Yaqui songs were recorded at Guadalupe village, near Phoenix, AZ., in 1922. These Indians were citizens of Mexico and preserved many of their tribal customs including the Deer Dance. The songs of this dance are concerning the actions of various birds and animals but one is of special interest. The words were translated, "The bush is sitting under the tree and singing." The interpreter explained the last word was correctly translated as "singing," but that it referred to the putting forth of magic power. The bush, "sitting under the tree," shared in the power that pervades the universe.

It is customary for a man to wear or carry some article connected with his dream which shows its general subject, though he may not reveal all its details. A song of the Sioux Sun Dance mentions the wearing of certain symbols as a requirement of a dream. This song was recorded by Red Bird on the Standing Rock Reservation, North Dakota, in 1912. It was sung at a Sun Dance by the Intercesser, during one of the periods when the dancers rested, the people listening attentively. In explanation, Red Bird said that the Intercesser, in his dream, saw the rising sun with rays streaming out around it. He made an ornament which represented this and wore it. The ornament is a hoop with feathers fastened lightly to it. The hoop represents the sun and the feathers fastened to it are the feathers of the eagle, which is the bird of day; the crane, which is the bird of night; and the hawk, which is the bird of prey. The words were:

(First rendition)
The sun is my friend,
a hoop it has made me wear,
an eagle it has made me wear.

(Second rendition)
The moon is my friend,
a crane it has made me wear,
a hawk it has made me wear.

The use of music in the treatment of the sick has been a subject of special study by the writer in many tribes, and the songs used in such treatment have been recorded, together with the dreams in which they had their origin. The man who recorded the largest number of such healing songs was Eagle Shield, a Sioux who recorded nine songs that he used in his own practice. His specialty was the treatment of fractures, and he recorded a song that he sang four times "while getting ready to apply the medicine." Most of his remedies for adults were received from bear, and one song contained the words "bear told me about all these things." Certain procedures were often part of his treatment and one of his songs was sung only three times when administering a certain herb. His remedies for children were received from the badger and there were no songs with these remedies.

A study of the dream song in many tribes reveals the place that song occupied in the life of the American Indians. They had their songs with games, dances, legends, and folk stories but those phases of their music were apart from its chief function — their communication with the supernatural, through which they believed that they could secure aid in every undertaking.

BIBLIOGRAPHY

Blackbear, Ben-Theisz, R.D. *Songs and Dances of the Lakota* 1976

Densmore, Frances *The American Indians and Their Music* 1926

Densmore, Frances *The Belief of the Indian in a Connection between Song and the Supernatural* 1953

Densmore, Frances *Technique in the Music of the American Indian* 1953

Evans, C. Scott *Northern Traditional Dancer* no date given

Ewing, Douglas *Pleasing the Spirits* 1982

Haffenreffer Museum *Hau Kola* 1980

Hunt, W. Ben *The Complete How-to Book of Indiancraft* 1942

Mason, Bernard S. *Drums, Tom-toms, and Rattles* 1938

Mason, Bernard S. *Dances and Stories of the American Indian* 1944

Missouri Arts Council *Sacred Circles* 1976

Powers, William K. *War Dance* 1990

Russell, Sharman Apt *Songs of the Flute Player* 1991

Scriver, Bob *The Blackfeet* 1990

THE TECHNIQUE OF NORTH AMERICAN INDIAN BEADWORK
by MONTE SMITH

This informative and easy to read book was written by noted author and editor Monte Smith and contains complete instructions on every facet of doing beadwork. Included is information on selecting beads; materials used (and how to use them); designs, with a special emphasis on tribal differences; step-by-step instructions on how to make a loom, doing loom work and the variations of loom work; applique stitches including the lazy stitch, "crow" stitch, running stitch, spot stitch and return stitch; bead wrapping and peyote stitch; how to make rosettes; making beaded necklaces; and, a special section on beadwork edging. There is also a section of notes, a selected bibliography and an index.

The book features examples and photos of beadwork from 1835 to the present time from twenty-three Tribes.

Anyone interested in the craft work of the North American Indian will profit from owning this book.

NORTH AMERICAN INDIAN BURIAL CUSTOMS
by
DR. H. C. YARROW

Edited by Monte Smith, this informative book was written for the Smithsonian Institute, Bureau of Ethnology, in 1879 while Dr. Yarrow was Acting Assistant Surgeon General of the United States.

Based on all available primary sources and personal research, the book describes and illustrates in detail all of the mortuary customs from inhumatio, deposition, surface burial, cremation, aerial sepulture, aquatic burial and all of the customs pertaining to these practices.

The customs of all of the major Indian Nations are explored and described in great detail and with first-hand authority.

This book of 96 pages has 47 illustrations and will be invaluable to anyone interested in the traditions and culture of the American Indian. Well researched and well written.

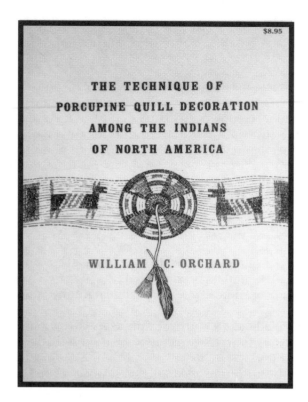

THE TECHNIQUE OF PORCUPINE QUILL DECORATION AMONG THE INDIANS OF NORTH AMERICA
By
WILLIAM C. ORCHARD

Written in 1917 by William C. Orchard, this book quickly established itself as a classic and remains today the definitive authority on the art of porcupine quillwork among the Indians of North America; a craft that is unique to this culture.

The book is fully illustrated and features a color center section of examples of the art form. The plates and diagrams show every facet of quillwork from plaiting through wrapping. The step-by-step instructions are easy to follow for the craftsperson and the pictures and text make this a treasure for anyone interested in the craftwork of Native Americans.

There are 84 pages and 30 illustrations in this 6" x 9" format and this is the fourth printing of the *Eagle's View*© edition in perfect bound.

CROW INDIAN BEADWORK
by
WILLIAM WILDSCHUT

A "descriptive and historical study" of the beadwork of the Crow Indian Nation. Between 1907 and 1916 Dr. Robert H. Lowie made repeated visits to the Crow Agency Reservation to study their traditional customs and, as a result, published the first paper on Crow Indian beadwork. Based on this research, in 1918 Wm. Wildschut began to collect specimens among them for the Heye Foundation.

His work went far beyond merely collecting specimens. He asked questions from his Crow associates and in 1927 produced a manuscript for the Heye in which he concluded that "true Crow beadwork was not borrowed from the neighboring Western Sioux, nor from any other Tribe. It possessed a distinctive character of its own."

In 1957, Dr. John C. Ewers made further inquiries and this book was produced providing an illustrated description and history of *Crow Indian Beadwork* from the time of its first mention by the fur trader, Francois Larouque, in 1805.

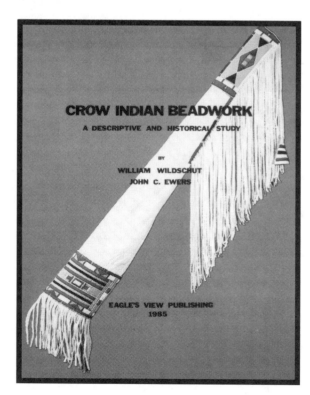

ETIENNE PROVOST:
Man of the Mountains
by
JACK B. TYKAL

Dr. Fred Gowans (*Rocky Mountain Rendezvous*) writes, in the introduction, that "the events of Provost's life represent a looking glass into the total history of the Rocky Mountain fur trade. It would have been very difficult to find a person closely associated with the beaver trade in the American West who did not know Etienne, but considered him one of the outstanding individuals of that era. From Santa Fe and Taos to the remote valleys of the Rocky Mountains and the executive offices of the giant fur companies in St. Louis, his name was known and recognized as one who knew and understood every facet of the business."

Written by noted scholar Jack Tykal, this book is a must read for anyone interested in Native Americans and the era of the mountain man. Both interesting and informative of this pivotal period on the Plains.

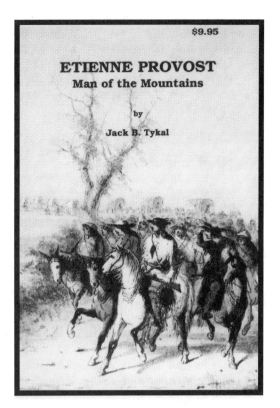

$9.95

ETIENNE PROVOST
Man of the Mountains

by

Jack B. Tykal

$7.95

TRADITIONAL INDIAN

CRAFTS

BY

MONTE SMITH

TRADITIONAL INDIAN CRAFTS
by
MONTE SMITH

Includes complete illustrated instructions on all of the basics of leather, bone and feather crafts.

Projects described are the bear claw necklace, imitation bone hairpipe breastplate, hairpipe breastplate, Sioux choker, ermine tail choker, tube & abalone choker, tube style choker, claw & hairpipe choker, single claw choker, mountain man choker, medicine pouch, small leather pouch, quilled medicine wheels, dance bell set, dance whistle, single feather, quilled single feather, dance bustle and warbonnet.

In addition, craft techniques described include porcupine quill wrapping, shaping feathers, how to size projects, using imitation sinew, how to antique bone, obtaining a "finished" look and hints on personalizing your craft projects.

This book is designed so that even the beginning craftsman can create authentic Indian crafts!

❑	**Eagle's View Publishing Catalog of Books**	B00/99	$3.00
❑	**The Technique of Porcupine Quill Decoration**/Orchard	B00/01	$9.95
❑	**The Technique of North American Indian Beadwork**/Smith	B00/02	$10.95
❑	**Techniques of Beading Earrings** by Deon DeLange	B00/03	$8.95
❑	**More Techniques of Beading Earrings** by Deon DeLange	B00/04	$8.95
❑	**America's *First* First World War: The French & Indian**	B00/05	$8.95
❑	**Crow Indian Beadwork**/Wildschut and Ewers	B00/06	$8.95
❑	**New Adventures in Beading Earrings** by Laura Reid	B00/07	$8.95
❑	**North American Indian Burial Customs** by Dr. H. C. Yarrow	B00/09	$9.95
❑	**Traditional Indian Crafts** by Monte Smith	B00/10	$9.95
❑	**Traditional Indian Bead & Leather Crafts**/ Smith/VanSickle	B00/11	$9.95
❑	**Indian Clothing of the Great Lakes: 1740-1840**/Hartman	B00/12	$10.95
❑	**Shinin' Trails: A Possibles Bag of Fur Trade Trivia** by Legg	B00/13	$7.95
❑	**Adventures in Creating Earrings** by Laura Reid	B00/14	$9.95
❑	**Circle of Power** by William Higbie	B00/15	$7.95
❑	**Etienne Provost: Man of the Mountains** by Jack Tykal	B00/16	$9.95
❑	**A Quillwork Companion** by Jean Heinbuch	B00/17	$9.95
❑	**Making Indian Bows & Arrows...The Old Way**/Doug Spotted Eagle	B00/18	$12.95
❑	**Making Arrows...The Old Way** by Doug Spotted Eagle	B00/19	$4.50
❑	**Hair of the Bear: Campfire Yarns & Stories** by Eric Bye	B00/20	$9.95
❑	**How To Tan Skins The Indian Way** by Evard Gibby	B00/21	$4.50
❑	**A Beadwork Companion** by Jean Heinbuch	B00/22	$10.95
❑	**Beads and Cabochons** by Patricia Lyman	B00/23	$9.95
❑	**Earring Designs by Sig: Book I** by Sigrid Wynne-Evans	B00/24	$8.95
❑	**Creative Crafts by Marj** by Marj Schneider	B00/25	$9.95
❑	**How To Bead Earrings** by Lori Berry	B00/26	$10.95
❑	**Delightful Beaded Earring Designs** by Jan Radford	B00/27	$8.95
❑	**Earring Designs by Sig: Book II** by Sigrid Wynne-Evans	B00/28	$8.95
❑	**Craft Cord Corral** by Janice S. Ackerman	B00/30	$8.95
❑	**Classic Earring Designs** by Nola May	B00/32	$9.95
❑	**How To Make Primitive Pottery** by Evard Gibby	B00/33	$8.95
❑	**Plains Indian & Mountain Man Arts and Crafts** by C. Overstreet	B00/34	$13.95
❑	**Beaded Images: Intricate Beaded Jewelry** by Barbara Elbe	B00/35	$9.95
❑	**Earring Designs by Sig-Book III: Celebrations** by S. Wynne-Evans	B00/36	$9.95
❑	**Techniques of Fashion Earrings** by Deon DeLange	B00/37	$9.95
❑	**Beaded Images II: Intricate Beaded Jewelry** by Barbara Elbe	B00/38	$9.95
❑	**Picture Beaded Earrings for Beginners** by Starr Steil	B00/39	$9.95
❑	**Plains Indian & Mountain Man Arts and Crafts II** by C. Overstreet	B00/40	$12.95

At your local bookstore or use this handy form for ordering :

EAGLE'S VIEW PUBLISHING READERS SERVICE, DEPT NAM-897
6756 North Fork Road - Liberty, Utah 84310

Please send me the above title(s). I am enclosing $_____ (Please add $3.50 per order to cover shipping and handling.) Send check or money order - no cash or C.O.D.s please.

Ms./Mrs./Mr. _____

Address _____

City/State/Zip Code _____

Prices and availability subject to change without notice. Allow 2 to 3 weeks for delivery.